GARDENING

In No Time

GARDENING

50 step-by-step projects and inspirational ideas

In No Time

TESSA EVELEGH

Photography by Debbie Patterson

CICO BOOKS

LONDON NEW YORK

Published in 2011 by CICO Books
an imprint of Ryland Peters & Small Ltd
519 Broadway, 5th Floor, New York NY 10012

www.cicobooks.com

10 9 8 7 6 5 4 3 2 1

A CIP catalog record for this book is available from the
Library of Congress.

ISBN 978 1 907563 25 6

Printed in China

Project editor: Dawn Bates
Text editor: Sarah Hoggett
Designer: Christine Wood
Photographer: Debbie Patterson

contents

introduction

Everyone loves a beautiful garden: the lush swathes of plants and flowers, the heady aromas, the gentle sound of birdsong and busy insects collecting sweet nectar, the sheer abundance of ripening fruits and vegetables. The natural beauty and variety of plants has always fascinated me, ever since my family returned from the exotic, tropical Far East to abundant Britain in springtime. But because we moved every two years, the luxury of long term-garden planning was never an option. Yet although there may have been a feeling of quick turnover, my love of plants and gardens was born.

As an adult, I have been able to build a couple of gardens of my own over the years, but while I've always had an overall long-term master plan, I've been impatient for instant impact while saplings grew to trees, shrubs thickened out, and the framework developed. The answer, I've found, is to take some of the basic principles of gardening (structure, color, texture, bulk)

and to translate them into eye-catching features that can be created in an hour or two for instant interest, then enjoyed all summer or longer. Over the years, these become part of the general character of the garden, creating a living journal of the seasons and of the memorable times you've spent outside with family and friends.

The key is not to be too precious and to take tips from the experts: if part of the garden has faded, add a confident splash of color by putting in a swathe of three or more of the same variety; introduce some freestanding interest or structure with a pillar, piece of furniture, trellis, or container. That is what this book is about: 50 quick projects that will add zest, a sprinkling of wit, or a touch of the theatrical to your garden.

OPPOSITE: *A reproduction Victorian birdcage makes a delightful container, which looks pretty hanging from a tree, positioned outside the front of the house or even placed on the garden table.*

LEFT: *Make your own hanging basket from ticking oilcloth— so pretty and so easy, especially if you bed the plants into a plastic garden pot first and simply lower it into the cloth before hanging.*

1 creative containers

Packed with instant color and positioned just where you want them, containers are hard to beat when it comes to gardening in no time. Purists will tell you that April's the time to be pushing your cart around the garden center in search of the best young bedding plants. Choose the ones that are just beginning to show color, so that you can be sure of your palette and color combinations. Add some good-quality potting mix that comes packed with nutrients to give the young plants a strong start, add slow-release fertilizer, and water-retaining gel to help you get through the summer. Allow yourself about half an hour to plant up. Then, with a little TLC through the summer, your containers will reward you by blossoming into vibrant, tumbling color.

But it has to be said that, first, we're not all purists, and second, some of us forget about that early planting. Suddenly, summer is upon us; everyone else's house front and patio are lush with summer blooms, and ours is, well, just a little bit sad. No problem. As the summer progresses, more mature plants are available in the garden centers; and although this timing is not ideal for the plants, these can be put together for instant effect. With the warmer weather and vigilant watering, they'll soon fill out into tumbling gorgeousness.

rusty tones

● *15 minutes*

Color and shape are the main keys to putting together successful container combinations. It doesn't have to be complicated: a container filled with just one type of plant can provide great impact. These fabulous Mexican hat flowers, with their rust-colored petals dancing like skirts on top of fine, wiry stalks, are far too special to be hidden among other varieties. Planting them in an old, rusted urn emphasizes their coppery hues. The classical, architectural shape of the urn also brings form to the whole arrangement, providing a foil for the rather untidy plant. One on its own makes a charming alternative to the more usual containers planted with summer bedding; two —one on either side of a door or pathway—would be a statement.

you will need

Urn

Mexican hat plant (*Ratibida columnifera* 'Red Midget') (zones 3–8)

Potting mix

Crocks

Water-retaining gel

2 handfuls of 1-in (20-mm) blue slate

AFTERCARE

Position in a sheltered site in full sun. Water well from April through August.

OPPOSITE, RIGHT: *Make a feature of these striking and unusual Mexican hat flowers, with their coy, turned-down petals, by planting them in a metal urn that complements their rich, rusty tones.*

1 Water the plant thoroughly to allow the mixture to become wet through. If the mix has been allowed to dry out, stand the plant in water for an hour or so before you plant it in the urn.

2 Place a large pebble, a piece of slate, or a piece of terracotta crock in the bottom of the urn over the drainage hole. This will prevent the mix from seeping out.

3 Using a trowel, put a layer of potting mix in the bottom of the urn. Add some water-retaining gel, following the manufacturer's instructions.

4 Carefully remove the plant from its pot and, without damaging or disturbing the roots, plant it in the urn. Next, fill around the root ball with potting mix, pressing it in firmly with your fingers to fill any air spaces.

5 Dress the top of the mixture with small pieces of slate to serve as a mulch. The blue tones of the slate make an attractive contrast with the rusty urn. If you don't have any slate, pebbles are a good alternative.

filigree flair

● *1 hour*

Fabulous seasonal color, planted into pretty window boxes, immediately lends personality to the front of the house. You can use traditional troughs on a variety of pots or source a container with a difference to fit your windowsill. This delicate-looking, metal window box is the perfect foil for light, ballerina-like begonias, which will happily bloom from late spring right through the summer in return for minimal care. A lining of luscious green moss sets off the lacelike metal container, while the high back provides a frame for the plant. Variegated ivy softens the whole arrangement, but please note that it is hardy only in very warm zones—9–11.

you will need

Metal window box

Pincushion moss—enough to cover the base, sides and top of the window box

Black-plastic trash bag

Scissors

Potting mix

1 *Begonia boliviensis* 'Million Kisses Elegance' (zones 9–11)

6 small, variegated English ivies

OPPOSITE: *A delicate, filigree-effect, metal window box sets off the dancing flowers of this light, airy begonia.*

RIGHT: *'Million Kisses Elegance', with its gently tumbling habit, is a particularly pretty begonia, which works well set in front of tall, narrow windows.*

1 Water all the plants and allow them to drain. Use the pincushion moss to line the window box, starting by laying it green side down in the bottom.

2 Now line all the sides of the box, placing the pincushion moss green side out and firmly pressing it into position.

3 Cut a black-plastic trash bag to generously line the window box and cut some small holes into it at 6-in (15-cm) intervals to act as drainage holes.

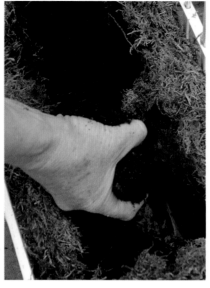

4 Lay the black plastic in the window box, spreading it out so that it lines the bottom and all the sides.

5 Using your hands, spread a layer of container potting mix in the bottom of the window box.

6 Carefully remove the begonia from its pot and place it in the center of the window box.

7 Add the ivies around the begonia, letting them trail to the front and sides of the window box.

8 Using a trowel, fill around the plants with potting mix, carefully but firmly pressing it in with your fingers.

9 Place pincushion moss on the surface to cover the mix and to serve as a mulch, preventing the mixture from drying out.

10 Generously water the finished container. This helps to settle the potting mix, filling in any air gaps.

ABOVE: *Begonias are a brilliant choice for containers, as they go on producing their delightful, ballerina-like flowers right up to the first frost.*

AFTERCARE

Position in sun or light shade, and water regularly in dry spells. Liquid feed every two weeks with a high-potash fertilizer. Protect from frost over winter or bring indoors.

antique chic

● *30 minutes*

Secondhand stores can often turn up special finds: this antique French, cast-iron trough was found in a mirror specialist dealer's and picked up for a song. Its exquisite, curvy lines bring a touch of Parisian chic to any windowsill. No matter that the bottom had rotted away—plants can be bedded down in a new container inside it. Here, the French theme has been carried through by planting the trough with lavender, complemented by the delicate mauve and pink of the nemesias. Positioned on a windowsill, patio, or garden table, it brings instant fragrance to the garden.

you will need

Antique or secondhand container

New trough, to fit inside the main container, in a similar color

Potting mix

Water-retaining gel

2 Hidcote lavenders (*Lavandula angustifolia* 'Hidcote') (zones 5–8)

3 *Nemesia*—a purple-blue variety such as **Golden Eye**

1 Gather together the containers, plants and potting mix. Inner containers made of terracotta could be painted if necessary.

2 Thoroughly water all the plants and allow to drain. Half-fill the inner trough with mix, and add water-retaining gel.

3 Place the three nemesias at the front of the trough, spacing them evenly and leaving room at each end for them to spread.

4 Position the lavender plants behind the nemesias.

5 Fill any gaps with potting mix and press it down well with your fingers.

6 Gently lower the new, inner trough inside the old one.

AFTERCARE

Place in a sunny position and keep watered throughout the warm weather. The lavender flowers last into early summer, after which they begin to dry out. Nemesia does best in cool summers; if your summers are hot, you might choose ageratum or phlox instead.

OPPOSITE: *Lavender brings height to the planting, while the lower and denser purple-blue nemesias add color impact.*

birdcage brilliance

● *30 minutes*

Anything with drainage holes can be drafted in as an effective planter—and if it doesn't have holes, you can always make them! Birdcages are particularly attractive, providing a charming structure for climbing plants to weave through with their tendrils and introducing an architectural element to any outside space. You can find reproduction Victorian birdcages like this one in garden centers, florists, and gift shops. Trawl secondhand and antique stores, and you might even get lucky and find an original! Not all birdcages are suitable as containers, as many old ones have only a tiny opening. Those with hinged tops that can be lifted, such as this one, make for much easier planting and watering. You'll need to place a container inside the birdcage to hold the potting mixture. The planting shown here is a temporary one.

ABOVE: *Over the course of the summer, Surfinia petunias produce lush trails of flowers, which will continue right into the fall if you deadhead them. This one may be named 'Yellow', but it produces a mass of creamy blooms.*

you will need

Birdcage
Shallow terracotta dish to fit
Terracotta crocks
Potting mix
Water-retaining gel
Slow-release fertilizer granules
Petunia Surfinia Series 'Yellow'
2 *Callibrachoa* million bells series

OPPOSITE: *When you have a pretty container such as this reproduction Victorian birdcage, you can keep the plant combination simple. Here, creamy, trailing* Surfinia *petunias fill out the birdcage and will eventually spread out through the bars of the cage like a flirty summer dress. The million bells (*Calibrachoa*), with their purple-tinged petals, lend extra impact to the color palette.*

1 Water the plants and let them drain. If the soil has been allowed to dry out or if the plant is root-bound, soak it in a bucket of water for at least an hour and allow to drain before planting.

2 Place the terracotta dish in the birdcage and place broken crocks over the drainage holes.

3 Part fill the planting mix with compost specifically designed for hanging baskets and other containers. This is formulated to include extra fertilizers to give the plants a good, healthy start.

4 Add water-retaining gel, following the manufacturer's instructions. This gel swells when it comes into contact with water and helps to prevent the potting mix from drying out during hot spells.

5 Add slow-release plant feed, following the manufacturer's instructions. This helps to keep the mix packed with nutrients all summer long for a full, lush show of blooms.

6 Place the *Petunia* Surfinia at one side of the dish, letting it trail over the side. For instant impact, we chose a mature, already flowering petunia, but even if you plant a smaller one, it will soon catch up, producing a froth of blooms all summer long.

7 Fill any spaces with the two *Callibrachoa* million bells, carefully removing the plants from their pots to avoid damaging their roots. Gently tuck them in next to the *Petunia* Surfinia for a pretty summer combination.

8 Fill between the plants and the edge of the dish and also any gaps between the plants with potting mix, pressing it down firmly with your fingers. Finally, water in the planted arrangement.

RIGHT: *Also known by the rather easier-to-remember name of million bells, Calibrachoa is a smaller "cousin" of the Petunia Surfinia, and so complements it well. With its gentle hint of pink tones, it adds dimension to the finished planting.*

AFTERCARE
Keep the container well watered. Check daily throughout the summer for deadheads and remove them, as this will encourage repeat flowering well into early fall.

pure fabrication

● *1 hour*

It's surprisingly easy to make your own containers, sometimes from unlikely materials. This hanging basket has been constructed with oilcloth made from traditional ticking, gathered together using braid threaded through large grommets. Planted with a raspberry-toned verbascum and variegated ivy, it makes a refreshing and pretty alternative to classic, moss-lined hanging baskets. Strong, waterproof, and readily available, oilcloth makes an ideal material, which is easy to handle. It's best to place the plants in the finished container still in their pots, as this gives structure to the cloth basket. If the plant looks a little pot-bound when you buy it, you may want to plant it in a larger pot first to give it growing room over the summer.

you will need

Oilcloth 24 in (60 cm) square
Grommet kit consisting of at least 10
½ in (10.5-mm) grommets and punching tool
Hammer
Sharp embroidery scissors
4½ yd (4.5 m) cotton braid
1 potted *Verbascum* 'Cherry Helen' (zones 5–9)
Variegated English ivy

OPPOSITE: *Make a hanging "basket" from colored oilcloth for a fresh and pretty alternative to traditional wire. This neutral ticking with raspberry-colored stripes perfectly complements the raspberry tones of the* verbascum.

RIGHT: *Braid threaded through grommets and tied in a knot holds the container together. The same braid is used for hanging.*

1 Fold the oilcloth into quarters. Using your fingers, make a hard crease to mark the center of the cloth.

2 Use a hammer to mark the center of the cloth. In lighter fabrics, this would make the eyelet hole. On sturdy oilcloth, this is more likely to simply make a mark on the fabric.

3 Using small, sharp-pointed embroidery scissors, neatly cut out the hole.

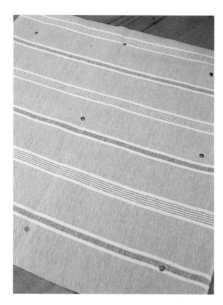  

4 In the same way, make holes 3 in (8 cm) in from the edge of the fabric along the two center creases and also 5 in (12 cm) in from each corner.

5 Assemble the two halves of each grommet on the punching tool, following the manufacturer's instructions.

6 Use the hammer to fix the grommets into position in each prepared hole.

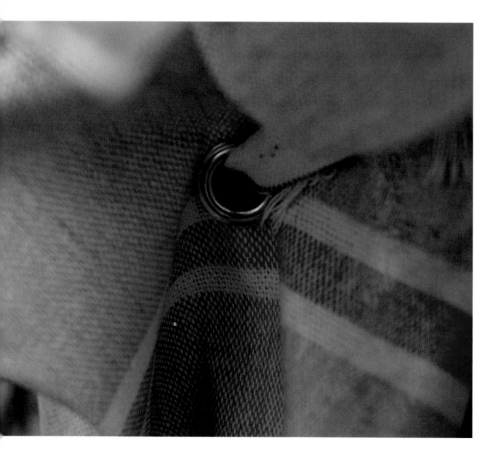 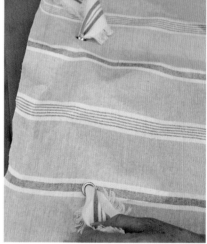

7 Starting in the center of one side, thread the braid in and out of the holes around the edge of the oilcloth. (Do not thread it through the center drainage hole.)

LEFT: *Oilcloth is made of hardwearing cloth by treating it with a thick, transparent, waterproof coating.*

8 Place the potted verbascum in the center of the oilcloth and draw up the sides. Leaving the same amount of braid overhanging at each end, tie the ends together in a square knot at the front.

9 To tie a square knot, take the left end of the braid over the right and bring it up underneath; then take the new right end of the braid over the left and bring it up in the loop that has formed between the two ends. Pull tight. Cut off the excess braid from each side.

10 Plant some variegated ivies in the pot with the verbascum, allowing them to trail over the sides. Make sure you press the compost in firmly around them, so that they are held in position.

11 Cut each piece of excess braid in half lengthways. Thread one end of a piece through a corner eyelet. Tie tightly. Repeat with the other three pieces, tying one piece of braid at each corner.

12 Gather up all four pieces of braid and tie together in a firm knot at the top to make a support for hanging the "basket".

AFTERCARE
Keep the planting well watered over the summer. It should drain through its own container and out through the drainage hole in the center. Do not overwater. Remove faded flower stems to encourage more flowers. The ivy will thrive with very little encouragement. If the *verbascum* becomes very tired looking, replace it with an alternative, such as trailing *Verbena*.

mosaic pot toppers

● *1 hour*

Pebble mosaics bring a charming touch to any garden, but they can be complicated to execute. Draw your inspiration from pebble and stone mosaics in grand gardens and use the ideas to make pretty mulching on potted plants. This is a striking way of decorating the tops of pots planted with trees or plants with narrow stems, such as cordylines or palms. This planting features a lovely Japanese maple—a plant that really needs an effective mulch; for if the soil is allowed to dry out, scorched leaves will result. Choose pebbles, slate, gravel, or even shells that complement the pot, then plan a simple design. It works best where there is plenty of contrast, so aim to combine dark colors—pieces of charcoal gray or black—with paler tones.

you will need

Large container
Good garden loam
Small bag sharp sand
Small bag pale gravel
Small bag 2-in (40-mm) black slate
1 Variegated maple (*Acer palmatum* 'Asahi-zuru') (zones 6–9)

OPPOSITE: *Simple mosaics bring interest to container plantings of trees and plants.*

LEFT: *You can use any contrasting stone material to make miniature mosaics as pot toppers. This design is made up of gravel and small slate chips. You could also use contrasting pebbles.*

1 Water the tree and allow to drain. If the soil has been allowed to dry out or if the plant is pot-bound, soak it in a bucket of water for at least an hour and allow to drain before planting.

2 Use a piece of slate to cover the drainage hole. Add enough soil to support the root ball, leaving about 4 in (10 cm) from the rim to allow for top dressing, the mosaic, and watering space.

3 Gently remove the maple from its pot, being careful not to damage any of the roots. Place it in the center of the container, standing it on top of the soil layer. Check height, and adjust it if necessary.

4 Fill between the root ball and the sides of the pot with soil and press it down firmly all around with your fingers to make sure there are no remaining air spaces.

5 Now add a 1-in (2.5-cm) layer of sharp sand. This covers up the dark soil, while providing an excellent, smooth layer as a base for the mosaic.

6 Next, using your hands, add some pale-colored gravel. Adjust the pieces to create an even layer over the surface of the pot, making sure that the sand is covered.

7 Place small pieces of slate on the top of the gravel around the perimeter of the container. Try to choose pieces that are more or less the same size.

8 Now place a line of similarl-size slate pieces across the diameter of the pot, making sure that they sit comfortably on top of the gravel.

9 Lay two lines in each half, out from the center, to create a bicycle-spoke-style design. Alternatively, make concentric circles of contrasting stones.

AFTERCARE

Variegated Japanese maples are especially prone to scorched leaves, caused by being put in too sunny or too windy a position or by the roots being allowed to dry out—all of which prevent the leaves from taking up all the moisture they need. They prefer shade or dappled sunlight, in a position sheltered from the wind. Water twice a day during the hottest months and re-pot in March every three to four years before the new growth appears. Give them a feed once the new leaves begin to emerge.

OPPOSITE: *Maples have traditionally been planted near water in Japan. Here, the finished planting looks exquisite situated on the edge of a lily pond.*

shell style

● *5 minutes*

Nature herself can provide pretty and imaginative containers. Alpines, which are used to tucking themselves in-between rocks or in cracks in walls, can be given surprisingly compact homes. You can, for example, make use of large shells or driftwood. However, you will need to provide plenty of drainage, as these plants don't like getting their roots too wet. This delicate, white-flowered, variegated *Silene* looks fabulous tumbling out of a giant clamshell. Set several in a line along a wall for greater impact. You could even create a whole montage by teaming it with a pretty oregano planted into an enamel bucket (see page 32).

you will need

Large clamshell
Handful of gravel
Potting mix
1 *Silene uniflora* 'Druett's Variegated' (zones 4–9)

ABOVE: *The pretty, little, white, bell-like flowers of Silene will cascade delightfully over the side of the shell from late spring right through until August.*

OPPOSITE: *The graphic undulations of large clamshells make an interesting container for small plants. However, as you cannot (and would not want to) drill drainage holes through the shell, make sure that you do not overwater the plants.*

1 Water the plant well and allow to drain. Put a layer of gravel in the bottom of the shell to allow drainage. Add potting mix. Carefully remove the plant from its pot and plant in the shell. Add more gravel as a mulch.

AFTERCARE

Place in a sunny position. Water occasionally to prevent the soil from drying out. Do not overwater.

buckets of color

● *15 minutes*

A traditional enamel bucket planted with oregano and mulched with emerald-green glass makes a confident combination. A useful potting-shed standby, glass mulch is available from good garden centers and will brighten any planting. The pretty *Origanum* 'Kent Beauty' shown here teams well with the *Silene* shown on the previous page, its tumbling, shrimplike flowers perfectly complementing the *Silene*'s white bells trailing from its shell. The containers (a bucket and a shell) imply a seaside theme, transforming the group into a little montage. The plants work well together for another reason: they both thrive in dry conditions.

you will need

Enamel bucket
Masking tape
Large nail
Hammer or mallet
Origanum 'Kent beauty' (zones 5–10)
Gravel
Potting mix
Green glass mulch

1 On the bottom of the bucket, stick a piece of masking tape in the place where you'd like to make the first drainage hole. Using a sharp implement, such as a large nail, and a hammer, make the hole. Repeat to make 6–8 drainage holes.

2 Water the plant well and allow it to drain. Put a layer of gravel in the bottom of the bucket to improve the drainage, then add potting mix. Remove the oregano from its pot and plant it in the bucket.

3 Fill around the root ball with potting mix, pressing it in firmly with your fingers. Sprinkle a layer of green glass mulch on top of the mix around the plant.

AFTERCARE

Place in a sunny, wind-protected position and water moderately. The *Origanum* is semi-evergreen and will not only survive, but continue to look pretty, through the early part of mild winters, as the petals dry out for lasting beauty. Where winters are cold, provide protection. When new shoots appear in the spring, cut back last year's growth and fertilize for a pretty summer display.

OPPOSITE: *A green glass mulch complements, rather than overwhelms, this delicate-looking plant because of its translucent quality.*

striped sensation

● *Half a day (including drying time); 2 hours "hands-on" time*

Create your own interesting containers by buying inexpensive terracotta pots at the local garden center, then adding a little paint. Solid colors always work well and can be used to team with the plants for impact in the garden. Even the artistically challenged can manage an allover tone. But you can do so much more than that, even if you're not confident with a paintbrush. The trick is to use masking tape to create stripes and simple shapes that can be repeated over the container. Allowing the terracotta to show through lends smart contrast. You can either make evenly sized stripes, as shown here, or, if you want more color, mask off more of the terracotta to make thinner sections. This basic stylized leaf motif can be used within stripes of different colors to create a sophisticated look for next to nothing. The same design has been painted in pale turquoise and taupe for vibrant verbenas, and aquamarine and battleship gray for more sculptural sedums.

you will need

Inexpensive terracotta pot
Measuring tape
Pencil
Masking tape
Small paintbrush
Primer
Latex paint in colors of your choice
Adhesive address labels
1 plant of your choice
Potting mix
Water-retaining gel
Slow-release fertilizer

OPPOSITE: *Purple verbena looks stunning tumbling from its rim of the pot*

1 Five stripes of any width always make a pleasing design, so start by measuring around the rim of the pot and dividing by five. Use a pencil to mark those points. Do the same at the bottom of the pot. Now work out how wide you want to make the stripes. Divide the figure by half and measure out to the left of each pencil mark by this amount and then to the right. These points will be the edges of the colored stripes. Line up the edge of the masking tape with the measured-out marks, starting at the bottom and pulling the tape up to the top and over into the inside of the pot.

2 Using a small paintbrush, paint the areas that are to be the colored stripes (that is, the areas between the strips of masking tape) with primer. Allow to dry.

3 Meanwhile, prepare the leaf shapes. Measure the height of the pot and take away 2 in (5 cm) to allow for spaces between the motifs. Divide the remainder by three. This will be the length of the middle motif. Add ½ in (1 cm) to the length for the top motif and take away ½ in (1 cm) for the bottom motif. Cut strips of adhesive address labels to half the width of the stripes. This will be narrower for the bottom motif and wider for the top one. Mark on the labels the relevant lengths of the motifs (see above) and hand draw the half-leaf motif shape on this.

4 Fold two labels back to back so that you can cut out both halves of the motif at once. Make one set of the three sizes of motif for each painted stripe in the same way.

5 Stick the motif shapes in position on the primed stripes.

6 Load the paintbrush with your chosen color, then dab the brush on waste paper to take off excess paint. Paint over the motif shapes.

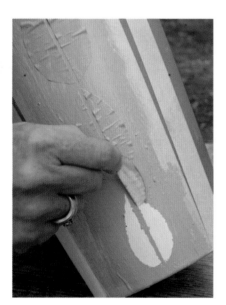

7 When the paint is completely dry, peel off the motif shapes, revealing the design. Finally, peel off the masking tape to finish.

8 Water the plant well and allow it to drain. Place a pebble or piece of crock over the drainage holes in the container. Part-fill the container with potting mix. Then add water-retaining gel, following the manufacturer's instructions.

OPPOSITE: *The smart gray and aquamarine stripes of the container perfectly set off this extrovert trailing sedum. The finished planting has a much more architectural appearance than the prettier, more feminine look of the verbenas on the previous page.*

9 Now add slow-release fertilizer in the quantity recommended by the manufacturer. Mix it well into the potting mix along with the water-retaining gel. Take the plant out of its container.

10 Lower the root ball into the container. Fill around it with potting mix, pressing it in firmly. Add a layer of mix, allowing watering space of about 1 in (2.5 cm). Water well.

AFTERCARE
Keep watered during the summer months, but allow the potting mix to dry out a little between waterings so that the surface is dry to the touch.

fig-leaf pots

● *3 hours (including drying time); 30 minutes "hands-on" time*

Another clever customizing idea is to take inspiration directly from nature, which has always been a treasure trove of wonderful, organic motifs. This bold design was easily executed using a leaf from a fig tree in the garden. By using a lively lime green over a quieter blue-green, you can guarantee it will look good in any garden and complement many plants. Planted with striking, evergreen, semi-variegated sisyrinchiums (here, "Aunt May"), it will look smart and structural all year round—perfect for marking the corner of a patio, or as a pair on either side of a pathway.

you will need

Square terracotta pot
Can of primer-sealer or paint-on primer
Paintbrush
2 sample cans of latex paint in contrasting colors
1 fig leaf
1 dishwashing sponge
2 *Sisyrinchium striatum* (zones 7–10)
Potting mix
Pebbles for mulching

OPPOSITE, LEFT *With large leaves such as fig leaves, you can wrap the design around the container corners for a quirky, fun design.*

OPPOSITE, RIGHT: *The strong, upright sisyrinchium stands free of the pot rim, perfectly showing off the design.*

AFTERCARE
Place in a sunny spot and keep watered, allowing soil to almost dry out before re-watering.

1 Try the fig leaves for size. Choose one that would give a pleasing design with several motifs on each side, allowing some to bend around the corners. Spray the whole pot with primer-sealer, or use the paint-on equivalent, and allow to dry.

2 Using a paintbrush, paint on the background color and allow to dry thoroughly.

3 Cut a small piece of sponge and dip it into the top color. Dab off the excess paint on waste paper. The drier the sponge, the better the results; if it's too wet, the paint may come off in blobs and may creep under the edge of the leaf.

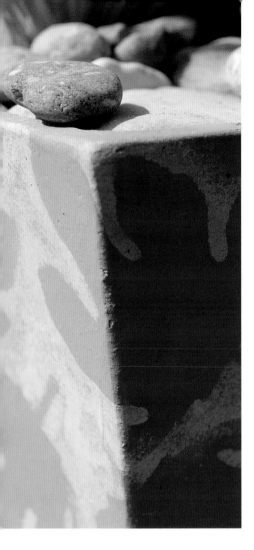

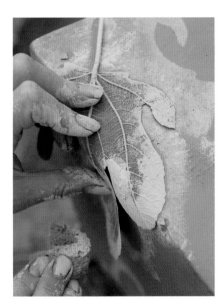

4 Hold the leaf firmly in position on the pot and, using the paint-loaded sponge, dab around the edges. Lift the leaf carefully, place in a new position, and repeat until the whole pot is covered. Plant up when dry and mulch.

lemon fizz

● *15 minutes*

Beverage and food cans make delightful containers. Choose ones with attractive graphics, or, like Andy Warhol, get inspired by cans of popular carbonated drinks, or cans of baked beans or soup. Beverage cans, in particular, are made of soft aluminum, which can easily be pierced for drainage holes. Food cans are somewhat sturdier, but still not difficult to perforate.

Most cans, of course, are of limited size, but you can create impact by massing them together. Use large olive oil cans, Mediterranean style, for bigger statements. Whatever you use, maximize the effect by teaming the hues of the plants with the colors used in the graphics. Here, Italian citrus drinks cans set off delightful *Cotula hispida* alpines, with their perky yellow buttons at the ends of antenna-like stalks. Even when the flowers die down, the cans serve as a great foil to the silvery cushions of fine leaves.

OPPOSITE: *Extrovert, yellow, button flowers "fizz" out from a carpet of soft leaves. The brightly colored citrus drink cans make witty, eye-catching containers for free.*

AFTERCARE
Place in a sunny position and water at intervals.

1 Using a bottle opener, make a drainage hole in the bottom of each can.

2 Use hand pruners to cut carefully into the top of each can.

3 Use scissors to cut the top off the can. The cut edge can be sharp, so protect yourself by taping on a narrow piece of duct tape once you've cut the top off.

4 Fill each can with potting mix and plant one alpine in each can.

2 instant impact

We all dream of lush swathes of color sweeping through our gardens. And indeed, this is exactly what we see in books and magazines and garden shows. So why is it that when we look out onto our own plot, it doesn't always measure up? The answer is often very simple. It might simply be a mid-season month: most gardens struggle to look gorgeous through the winter; more surprisingly, many have a bit of down time at the end of summer when everything's looking a little dried-out and overgrown. Or it might be that the garden is still not mature enough; most take about three years to mature.

The easiest instant-impact trick is to fill the gaps with swathes of current color. Here are some tricks of the trade. First: think bulk. Unless you're choosing a specimen plant, such as a tree or large shrub, plan to buy three, five, or even more of each plant. Second: think color. Choose a scheme for your border and make sure the newcomers fit in, whatever the season. So if you have a blue-ish border, you may choose mainly blue and purple plants—but pink may also work well. Third: think texture. This works for long-lasting leaves as well as for more fleeting flowers. For example, you might set large leaves with bold shapes, such as hostas, against small-leaved, neatly clipped box hedging.

Instant impact can also be provided by containers, where seasonal color can be concentrated and positioned exactly where it's needed—even within a flowerbed—then replenished with new color as the season changes.

daisy basket

● *30 minutes*

Pack a basket with golden marguerite daisies to lend a sunny splash in the garden exactly where you want it. Regularly snip off the deadheads, and you'll be rewarded with merry daisies all summer long. These have been planted into a generous open basket, which can easily be moved around and gives a rustic feel. It would make a delightful welcome near the front door or a pretty focal point on a garden table. Buy the marguerites while they are still young in packs of six or eight, and you'll have plenty to grow on into a lush display. You'll need to line the basket before planting up to prevent the potting mix from escaping through the cracks. Here, pincushion moss is used as a decorative mulch, to help retain the moisture during the hot summer months. As the season progresses, the marguerites will grow to cover this up.

you will need

Large basket about 20 in (50 cm) in diameter
Plastic trash bag
Scissors
Potting mix
Water-retaining gel (optional)
Slow-release fertilizer
12 small marguerite daisies (*Argyranthemum* 'Summersong Yellow') (zones 9–11)
Small quantity of pincushion moss

OPPOSITE: *These enchanting marguerite flowers, with their little petals arranged around generous centers, make an enchanting splash of instant color, which will last all summer long.*

1 First, water the plants and allow to drain. Next, you'll need to line the basket. Lay a black-plastic trash bag loosely into the basket and roughly cut it to size so that it generously fits the basket.

2 Next, you will need to make drainage holes. Snip little holes in the black plastic at about 6-in (15-cm) intervals.

3 Place a 2-in (5-cm) layer of potting mix in the basket, or more if you have a deep basket. Remove one marguerite plant from the pack and try it out for depth in the basket. If it is too low in the basket, add more potting mix. Take the plant out and add water-retaining gel and slow-release fertilizer, in the quantities recommended by the manufacturer, mixing them into the layer of potting mix.

4 Now plant the first marguerite in the center of the basket, carefully making a shallow hollow in the mixture to accommodate the root ball.

LEFT: *If you think the vegetable patch needs brightening up, slip the basket of marguerites in among the zucchini.*

5 In a similar way, plant marguerites on either side of the central plant, to create a line of plants across the basket.

6 Add half the remaining plants on one side of the central line and the other half on the other side. In this way, you will achieve an even distribution of plants. Use your hands to fill carefully between and around each plant with potting mix, pressing it in firmly with your fingers.

7 Finish off by placing pincushion moss over the bare potting mix around the edges to create a mulch. Thoroughly water the completed planting.

AFTERCARE
Position the container in full sun or partial shade. Keep the arrangement moist all summer, watering moderately. Deadhead regularly.

LEFT: *The striking* Cordyline Pink Passion *brings vivid color to this town garden. This one serves as the centerpiece for containers planted up for spring with bleeding hearts and violet pansies.*

pots up front

● *1 hour*

Vary the effect as the year progresses. Add interest and flexibility by planting up a pair of containers that complement each other, while providing a broader spread of plants for greater impact. This arrangement is centered around the striking *Cordyline* Pink Passion, which provides structure and color in warm months. In spring, the pink was picked out in the front container by arching branches of bleeding heart (*Dicentra spectabilis*). Both containers were underplanted with pretty, blue-purple pansies. Once the bleeding heart flowers and pansies were past their best, a selection of petunias and verbenas in pink, blue, and purple took their place to give vibrant colour until fall.

you will need

2 containers, roughly 16 in (40 cm) and 9 in (23 cm)
Potting mix
Water-retaining gel
Slow-release fertilizer
1 *Cordyline* **Pink Passion** (zones 8–11)
1 bleeding heart (*Dicentra spectabilis*) (zones 2–9)
12 winter pansies, *Viola* × *wittrockiana*

1 Using a watering can fitted with a rose, to avoid damaging the delicate flowers, thoroughly water all the plants, then allow them to drain.

2 Fill the containers with enough potting mix to support the root balls of the *Cordyline* and bleeding heart. Add water-retaining gel and slow-release fertilizer, in the proportions directed by the manufacturer, and mix in with the soil.

3 Position the *Cordyline* in the center of the taller container, carefully bedding it into the potting mix.

4 In the same way, carefully remove the bleeding heart from its pot and position it in the center of the lower container.

5 Carefully remove the pansies from their pots and arrange six around the *Cordyline*. Fill between and around all the plants with potting mix, carefully pressing it in with your fingers.

6 In the same way, remove the other six pansies from their pots and plant them around the bleeding heart, carefully pressing the mix around them with your fingers. Thoroughly water the finished containers.

AFTERCARE

Position in a sheltered, sunny position and water regularly. Do not allow to dry out. The *Cordyline* is hardy to zone 8 but will need to be moved into a greenhouse or sunroom during the winter in colder zones. Each year, it will shed lower leaves, and eventually it will reach a height of 5 ft (1.5 m). When the plants stops blooming, remove them from the container and plant in a border, or replant them in another container, ready for next year. Deadhead the pansies regularly.

impact planting

● *1 hour 30 minutes*

Think bulk for impact. Here, a row of white agapanthus makes a witty planting in a narrow bed at the side of a town garden. The bold white orbs dance merrily in full bloom above the wall from midsummer to fall, but in warm regions they bring interest in other seasons, too. During late spring and early summer, the flower spikes shoot up above the leaves, forming bold buds, and, in fall, the florets die back to striking, Sputnik-style seedheads. Native to southern Africa, some varieties of agapanthus are deciduous; others are evergreen and will survive very mild winters. This row was planted the year before these photographs were taken, but set back against the wall; the front of the bed was left with unattractively bare earth. In spring, nature obligingly filled the gap with common spurge, euphorbia's native woodland ancestor. Although it is often considered a weed, the spurge offered a pretty solution, which would, however, die back by fall. So, instead of pulling it out, it was decided to supplement it with cultivated euphorbias, chosen for their evergreen variegated foliage, bringing pale tones that complement the agapanthus flowers. By next spring, these will have filled out, taking the place of their native cousins.

you will need

Large evergreen agaphanthus such as 'Windsor Grey'—one per 12 in (30 cm) of bed

Euphorbia characias 'Tasmanian Tiger' – 2 for each agapanthus (zones 7–11)

Extra-rich garden loam

ABOVE RIGHT: *As summer progresses, the florets gradually open until eventually they become full-blown orbs.*

OPPOSITE: *A row of agapanthus, with their huge white blooms, brings witty charm to a city front-garden bed, but would look just as delightful in an informal garden. They are complemented by striking, variegated evergreen euphorbia.*

1 Choose a sunny position for planting. Water all the plants well and allow to drain. Dig a trench about 6 in (15 cm) deep, and fill with a 2-in (5-cm) layer of loam. Position the agapanthus crowns in the trench so they will be about 2 in (5 cm) below the surface. Fill in and around with soil, pressing in firmly around the crowns. Line up the euphorbias along the front of the bed to work out the spacing.

2 Once you're happy with the spacing, remove the euphorbias from their pots gently, to avoid damaging the root balls, and plant them in the prepared trench. Or if, as here, this is the second summer, plant them straight into the ground.

3 Mix soil and potting mix 50/50 and fill around the plants so that the root balls are completely bedded in, then press in firmly with your hands.

4 Thoroughly water in the newly planted plants to give them a good start.

AFTERCARE

Agapanthus

During the growing season, water regularly as necessary and liquid-feed every two weeks. In winter, there's no need to water. This border planting is really suited only to the warmest zones of the country. Even deciduous agapanthus is not very hardy. However, evergreen agapanthus can be grown individually in pots and partly submerged in the garden soil, then lifted up and brought indoors for the winter. A bit of extra work, but the splendid summer display is well worth it.

Euphorbia

In fall, wearing gloves (to protect against contact with the sap, which is a skin irritant), cut off faded flowers. In spring, mulch with well-rotted garden compost.

OPPOSITE: *Evergreen Euphorbia characias 'Tasmanian Tiger' keeps its pretty, variegated leaves throughout the year. In spring, these are topped by a froth of creamy-white flowers.*

color toners

● *1 hour*

Clever planting, like interior decoration, relies on several basic elements, one of which is color. One of the easiest ways to create impact is to keep it tonal. Decide on a basic hue and keep to its neighbors on the color wheel. By high summer, this wonderful pink rose was looking a little lonely. The solution was to complement it with annuals and perennials that ranged through the pink, red, and purple end of the spectrum to create a splash at the end of the garden. If you keep your plant choices to similar hues throughout the year, you can keep the vibrancy going, as new flowers take over when earlier blooms go past their best.

you will need

1 crimson snapdragon (*Antirrhyinum* spp.)
2 *Salvia sylvestris* 'Mainacht' (zones 5–8)
1 Petunia **Surfinia Purple**
Potting mix

OPPOSITE, RIGHT: *Spikes of deep crimson snapdragons lend a rich shadow to the stately purple salvia, providing a strong underplanting for the rose. Paler crimson-purple Surfinia petunias tumble over what was bare ground, and potted pelargoniums bring light to the scheme.*

1 Gather all the plants together. Water them thoroughly and allow to drain through before planting, to give all the plants a good start. Position the plants around the rose to make sure you are happy with the arrangement before you start digging.

2 Dig a planting hole of the correct depth for the root ball of the snapdragon, add some potting mix, and plant.

3 Dig a trench for the salvias. Put a layer of potting mix in the bottom of the trench to encourage good root development. Plant the salvias and fill the hole with more potting mix. Press it down with your foot to eliminate any air spaces.

4 In the same way, plant the Surfinia petunias in front of the salvias and snapdragon. Water in all the plants.

texture treats

● *1 hour*

One of the key secrets of stunning planting is to think texture as well as color. Set dramatic, large leaves against those that are small and more intricate. Here, huge smooth-sided, heart-shaped *Colocasia* leaves are set against serrated-edged leaves and a mass of pink daisies. It's a late-summer combination that will look stunning right into fall, as the larger Japanese anemones will continue the pink theme, even though the little pink *Coreopsis* will be past their best by the end of August. Try the same idea using readily available large-leaved plants, such as hostas or ornamental rhubarb (*Rheum palmatum*), or plant a fig tree to set off a border planting.

OPPOSITE: *The dark, heart-shaped leaves of Colocasia bring exotic impact to a simple border. Since this plant likes to keep its roots damp, it has been planted in a container that can be kept well watered. The bold, graphic shape of the pot lends extra emphasis and structure to the arrangement.*

ABOVE: *With their strongly ribbed undersides, the generous, heart-shaped leaves of Colcasia have a wonderfully sculptural quality.*

you will need

Japanese anemones (*Anemone japonica pink*) planted in the ground (zones 4–9)

2 *Coreopsis* 'Limerock Passion' planted in terracotta pots (zones 4–9)

Square faux-lead container

1 *Colocasia esculenta* 'Fontanesii' (zones 8–11)

Potting mix or muddy soil

Water-retaining gel

Large slate pieces for mulch

1 Pretty pink Japanese anemones, growing near a back door, make pretty cover but, with the introduction of some plants in containers, can become much more exciting for a season.

2 Place the potted *Coreopsis* to the side of the Japanese anemones to boost the color impact early in the season. (As the weeks go by, the *Coreopsis* will go past their best as the Japanese anemones come into their full autumn glory.)

3 Position the container in a suitable place to set off the Japanese anemones. Thoroughly water the *Colocasia* and allow it to drain.

4 Place a piece of crock in the bottom of the container to cover the drainage hole, then almost fill it with potting mix. Because *Colocasia* is a marginal plant, it likes to keep its roots wet, so it will do well in muddy, rather than free-draining sandy soil. If you are using potting mix, add plenty of water-retaining gel according to the manufacturer's instructions.

5 Gently remove the *Colocasia* from its pot, being careful not to damage its large, dramatic leaves. Once it is positioned at the correct height, carefully pack potting mix around the root ball, adding a layer of compost on the top about 1 in (2.5 cm) deep.

6 Mulch the top with pieces of slate to help retain the moisture. Large pieces have been used here to complement the large leaves: a thick layer of smaller slate pieces would work just as well.

AFTERCARE

Japanese anemones

Once established in a part-sunny, part-shady position, fully hardy Japanese anemones will be happy looking after themselves, as long as they're not allowed to dry out.

Coreopsis

Keep the *Coreopsis* watered, and deadhead the flowers to encourage repeat blooms.

Colocasia

Keep it well watered and it will grow to over 3 ft (1 m) with a spread of 2 ft (60 cm). Some colocasias are evergreen. This variety is deciduous, certainly in cooler climates, and can survive to just above freezing point, dying down in winter. Bring it under glass if there is any threat of frost, and the tuber should send out new leaves in the following spring. Some growers suggest bringing the plant in well before the first frosts so that you can keep it going. Note that although excellent for growing in containers, Colocasia tends to be invasive and has become established as a weed in hot regions such as Florida.

border rescue

● *1 hour*

Sometimes spring doesn't bring all you expected in the garden. Some of the denizens of your favorite perennial border may have fallen victim to a harsh winter, leaving bare earth where there should be lush greenery. This is not always a bad thing: think of it, instead, as an opportunity to update things. The most effective method is to put in a group of plants that complements the colors already there. A group of three or five of a single variety, which will grow into a swathe of color by the end of the summer, is much more effective than a lonesome plant, which could result in a "bitty" overall look. Here, last year's group of five perennial scabious, with their pretty blue petals, has been reduced to two. Instead of simply replacing the scabious, The more vibrant hues and upright form of *Primula vialii* have been used.

ABOVE: Primula vialii, *with their fabulous purple and red, pokerlike flowers, are happiest in boggy-like conditions, so keep them well watered at all times.*

you will need

5 *Primula vialii* (zones 5–9)
Potting mix
Slow-release plant fertilizer

OPPOSITE, RIGHT: *Statuesque purple and red* Primula vialii *complement the pretty blue scabious behind, invigorating the border. Both plants flower through most of the summer. If scabious is not readily available in your region, you might substitute Salivia superba 'May Night'.*

1 Water the plants and allow to drain. Position in a pleasing group in the space.

2 Dig a generous hole in the border in the position of one of the plants. Line it with potting mix. Add slow-release plant feed, as per the manufacturer's instructions.

3 Remove the plant from the pot, taking care not to damage the roots. Place it in the hole you have just dug.

4 Fill the hole with potting mix and press it in firmly around the plant with your fingers. Repeat steps 2–4 with the other four *Primula vialii* plants.

5 Water in the plants well to give them a good start.

AFTERCARE

Primula viallii are marginal bog plants, and will soon wilt and die if they are allowed to dry out. So keep them well watered all through the summer. Regularly deadhead the flowers for repeat flowers from late spring to midsummer.

raise the interest

● *15 minutes*

Spring's vigorous new growth brings the garden to life in an astounding display of vibrant greens and bold colors, but, in the early months everything is still somewhat low to the ground. The herbaceous perennials, if they have appeared at all, still have a few months to go before they reach their full, lush potential. The simple answer is to think of ideas that bring color to new levels in the garden. You could plant up baskets fixed to the wall, or find ways to raise up containers planted with spring interest. Here, a white foxglove fills the gap that will be sumptuously filled later in the year by the frothy, green-white blooms of *Hydrangea arborescens* 'Annabelle'. Standing the container on a vintage metal table is a charming solution.

ABOVE: *A spotted-throat, white foxglove provides height in a late spring and early summer planting. By placing it in a raised position, you can bring spring interest to parts of the garden that won't fill out until the summer.*

you will need

1 white foxglove (*Digitalis purpurea* f. *albiflora* 'Camelot White') (zones 4–8)
Potting mix
Water-retaining gel
Slow-release fertilizer

1 First, thoroughly water the foxglove and allow it to drain while you prepare the container.

2 If you are reusing an old pot, thoroughly scrub it out to make sure it is clear of any trace of any plant disease from a previous occupant or any mites or slugs that might damage the leaves or roots. Add a layer of potting mix, plus water-retaining gel and slow-release fertilizer, as per the manufacturer's recommendations.

3 Thoroughly mix the water-retaining gel and slow-release fertilizer into the potting mix.

RIGHT: *This pretty, container-planted, white foxglove has been raised up on a small table, filling a temporary space. The white flowers perfectly complement the emerging green-white blooms of the climbing hydrangea behind. As they die down, the place of the white foxglove flowers will be filled by the frothy blooms of the Hydrangea 'Annabelle aborescens'.*

AFTERCARE

Keep watered during dry periods and do not allow to die out. Cut down the first tall spire as soon as the flowers fade to encourage better blooms in the secondaries. You can leave the secondaries to go to seed for next year if you like. Most foxgloves die after flowering, but if you cut down the flowers, they may produce more green leaves in late summer, then re-surface in the autumn. Cut off any dead leaves and add more fertilizer.

4 Place the foxglove in the container; fill the sides, top with more potting mix, and press in firmly with your fingers. Thoroughly water in.

number crunchers

● *2 hours*

Grow your own house number and place it by the front door or gate for instant recognition. Bend wire into shape, then train a pretty, variegated ivy up it for a living number. Once it's in place, you can simply leave it to grow and thicken up with very little input from you. If your house number is in double figures or more, make up each number in its own container, then stand them together outside the house. For instant effect, invest in some long, trailing English ivy, which can be ordered from a florist if you can't get it in the garden center. You may find that what appears to be one large pot of trailing ivy is actually made up of several plants; check before you buy.

you will need

Terracotta container

Sturdy garden wire

Wire cutters

Small plastic flower pot to fit inside main container

Handful of pebbles or stones

Potting mix

6 long, trailing English ivies

1 If you have bought a large pot of long, trailing ivy, you may well find it is made up of up to 10 plants. If this is the case, take the plant out of its pot and plunge it into a bucket of water. By soaking the roots in this way, you will be able to disentangle the individual plants more easily without damaging the roots. Next, use the wire to create the number frame. For the number eight, the rim of the pot was used to create a smooth circle.

2 Make two similar wire circles, then wind another two thicknesses around each circle to strengthen them. Wire them a figure eight.

OPPOSITE: *Small-leaved, variegated ivy lends a light and pretty feel to this simple number topiary. Make the numbers big and bold, so that they can easily be seen from the street.*

3 Wind another length of wire along the bottom of the figure eight, leaving two long tails for fixing. Thread these two tails through the holes in the bottom of a small plastic pot, and bend the tails around the rim to the outside of the pot.

4 Place the pot upside-down in the bottom of the terracotta container, then add the pebbles around it to stabilize it.

5 Almost fill the container with potting mix. Next, take a single ivy plant and plant it into the container to one side of the wire figure.

6 Wind the ivy up the side of the wire number and plant another ivy into the container at the other side of the figure.

OPPOSITE: *A huge, potted foliage number is a witty way to mark your house. Choose an easy-to-care-for variegated ivy to keep it looking light and airy.*

7 Add in more ivies either side of the wire figure, and weave them up both sides of the figure, covering the wire and gradually building up a density of leaves. Water in the finished planting.

AFTERCARE
English ivy is very resilient and will tolerate almost any position throughout the year. Keep it well watered and do not let it dry out. As the ivy grows, entwine it around the wire to keep the overall shape of the number intact. If the ivy grows so thick that it threatens to obliterate the number, simply trim back some of the stems.

in-betweens

● *1 hour*

When July turns to August, the garden seems to go to sleep. The vibrant greens of early and midsummer turn from lush to overgrown and dry; the abundant blooms are past their best, and much seems to have gone to seed. Invest in something bright and beautiful from the garden center that will fill the gaps and complement the few blooms left to get you through to September or October, when dewy mornings and early autumn flowers bring the garden back to life. This is a stopgap, so there is no need to be subtle. Choose big and bold to celebrate the last of the summer heat.

you will need

Rudbeckia hirta 'Prairie Sun')
—one per 12 in (30 cm)
Potting mix

OPPOSITE: *Generous yellow* Rudbeckia hirta 'Prairie Sun', *bring vibrant life to a marigold and cornflower border.*

1 Bare earth is all too evident in the marigold and cornflower border after a prolonged summer's dry spell. The plan, for this bed, is to fill between the two rows with a vibrant but complementary flower. Measure the length to assess how many plants you will need. Allow one plant for each 12 in (30 cm).

2 Water the plants and allow to drain. Pick off any dead or damaged leaves. Arrange them along the outside of the border to assess the spacing. In the first position, dig a hole twice the size of the root ball. Place some potting mix in the bottom.

3 Place the plant in the hole so that the root ball is level with the soil surface. Fill around the root ball with a blend of potting mix and soil from the hole. Press it down firmly and water thoroughly.

AFTERCARE
Liquid-feed *Rudbeckia* when first planted, then water well, especially in dry weather. Although this was used to fill in late-summer gaps, it can be planted in spring, and it will reward you with months of showy flowers.

3 easycare

We all have different pressures on our time. Some of us can squeeze our gardening into a little-and-often time frame, while others prefer to take a single afternoon and tackle a bigger project—so long as it can then more or less look after itself. This is what this chapter is all about. You won't find projects that include the more tender garden denizens that might wither and die in a drought, or for fast growers that could get out of hand if they weren't pruned back, trained, or tied in. And you won't find ideas that might allow any space for weed growth. So what CAN the let-it-look-after-itself style of gardener do?

In general, a good plan is to think of "tough-cookie" plants that can survive droughts. Most have developed strategies to help them take root in tricky terrain or adverse conditions, and retain moisture—meaning they'll survive a fair amount of neglect. These plants include fleshy-leaved succulents; some highly scented plants protected by the essential oils in their leaves, such as lavender, rosemary, and thyme; and plants with thick, leathery leaves, such as olive trees, oleanders, and figs (though these won't survive harsh winters, so in cooler zones, you'll need to grow them in pots and bring them in during the coldest months). Some grasses, too, are perfectly modified to withstand arid or challenging conditions.

Another trick is to think of ways you can use plants that are happy all year round in whatever climate you happen to live in. We've used the example of English ivy, which can be used to make instant topiary. It comes in an astounding range of varieties, suited to many different climates. Look for local varieties that withstand local winters.

treat 'em mean

● *30 minutes*

Some plants positively thrive on neglect—and here's a fine example. Since this container of houseleeks (*Sempervivum*) was planted up two years ago, they have been left pretty much to their own devices on a hot and sunny front windowsill. In return for the occasional watering, they grew and thrived in a most satisfactory manner. Indeed, after eighteen months, they'd done so well and were so overcrowded that they had to be divided. Bravely, they then withstood an unusually cold English winter and rewarded us with an extraordinary display of flowers, sent out like fireworks from the basal rosettes. Houseleeks are often sold in trays of mixed varieties. They're always happy together, so choose your favorites, plant them, then sit back and enjoy.

you will need

A selection of houseleeks (*Sempervivum spp.*) (zones 5–8)

Container

Gravel for drainage

Gritty planting medium (made from roughly 50 percent soil-based potting mix, 25 percent sharp sand, and 25 percent gravel)

Washed shells for mulch

ABOVE: *Houseleeks send out an astonishing display of flowers in the summer, such as these vibrant red "stars".*

OPPOSITE: *Houseleeks make an excellent growing choice if you don't have time for gardening. Once planted, they'll get on with growing in return for very little TLC. With their fabulously extrovert flowers shooting out from fleshy basal leaves, when planted together in one container, they always make an intriguing display.*

1 Before planting, thoroughly water all the plants and leave them for a few hours to let them thoroughly drain through.

2 Houseleeks need good drainage; otherwise their roots and lower leaves rot. Fill the bottom of deep containers with gravel, then make up at least the top 6 in (15 cm) of gritty potting mix (see *you will need*, far left).

3 Arrange the houseleeks on top of the gritty soil, placing them fairly close together, but allowing a little room for growth.

4 Using a small trowel, carefully fill between and around each plant with the gritty soil, making sure that each one is well bedded in.

5 Press the soil down firmly with your fingers, adding more where needed. Position in a sunny spot and keep moist until established, then water sparingly.

OPPOSITE: Houseleeks look good from the moment they're planted. This is how the display looked when it was first planted two years ago. The plants didn't fill the container, so a mulch of shells was added.

ABOVE: Soft, neutral colors, such as these pinkish grays, make a sophisticated foil for the brighter houseleek flowers.

AFTERCARE

Rosettes that wither after flowering should be removed. Any gaps can be filled with offsets once their roots have developed. If the container becomes overcrowded, take out all the plants. Discard any withered ones and divide others, then replant, giving them space to expand.

grass spiral

● *Half a day (4–5 hours)*

If your lifestyle leaves you minimal gardening maintenance time, yet you still want to make a statement, plant a gravel garden. This one is simplicity itself: a spiral of blue grasses and black pebbles, which looks smart, graphic, and undeniably contemporary. Centered in front of a wooden bench painted in a similar color, it becomes a perfect focus for contemplation. These grasses were planted in an already graveled area, but it's not difficult to prepare the ground yourself (see Graceful Grasses, page 88). You'll need to take the dimensions to the local garden center, so they can work out the quantities. Many will deliver to the site.

ABOVE: *The architectural quality of the festucas' spiky blue-green leaves makes them an ideal choice for graphic designs such as this spiral, especially as they are evergreen, giving all-year garden interest.*

you will need

A graveled area (or black plastic mulch and gravel to cover the area to be planted)
Festuca glauca 'Elijah Blue' —at least 20 (zones 5–9)
Sharp knife
Organic soil conditioner or potting mix
50–60 black pebbles
6 or more skewers, tent pegs, or similar

1 Water all the plants and allow them to drain. If you want to create a graveled area from scratch, start by thoroughly weeding the area. Next, lay the plastic on the bare earth and top with gravel. The plastic both restricts weed growth and provides a base for the gravel.

2 Starting from the center, lay out the spiral with the plants still in the pots and adjust it until you are happy with the position, design, and spacing.

OPPOSITE: *The neat growing habit of festucas makes them an excellent choice for creating simple graphic designs, like this spiral. An "echo" of smooth gray pebbles lends emphasis to the design.*

3 Starting at the end of the spiral, working toward the middle, move the first two pots to one side and use the knife to cut through the plastic between the planting positions. Pin the plastic flaps back, using the skewers.

4 Use a spade to start digging a trench twice as wide as the root ball from one planting position to the next. Then, move the next two pots, cut the plastic as in the previous step, and pin that section back before digging the next section of the trench.

5 When you have dug the trench to accommodate about six plants, trowel in a layer of potting mix to give the plants a good, healthy start.

6 Place the first six grasses in position along the end of the spiral, then carefully fill between the plants with potting mix, pressing it in firmly with your fingers. Remove the skewers, fold the plastic back into position, and tuck it under the leaves of grass.

7 Continue in the same way with the next six plants, reusing the skewers to hold back the plastic as you dig the next section of the trench. Repeat until you reach the center of the spiral.

8 Use a plastic tub or bucket to fill in and around the plants with gravel for a smart overall effect.

9 Finally, lay the gray pebbles in a spiral, following the line of the grasses to finish the design.

AFTERCARE

Water the plants regularly until they are established, after which they can survive on less. After flowering, clip the plants lightly, and then clip again in spring. Divide and replant every two to three years.

smart all year

● *15 minutes*

Only Nature could paint such extraordinary colors as those found on echeverias. They're even more striking when they send out their extraordinary displays of flowers. And although these succulents are native to Latin America, a few varieties can survive frost down to 20°F (-7°C). Best of all, they blossom, grow, and provide a striking display with very little attention. In most zones, it's best to plant them in containers so that they can be brought inside for the winter. Make up a generous display to set on a patio, or plant up a pair of containers to stand on either side of a pathway.

you will need

Smooth-sided container
3 *Echeveria spp.* (zones 9–11)
Gritty planting medium (made from roughly 50 percent soil-based potting mix, 25 percent sharp sand, and 25 percent gravel)
Large gravel or pebbles for mulch

ABOVE: *This potted display makes a stunning focal point on the curved pathway of a lush herbaceous garden, bringing a splash of color.*

1 Water the plants and let them drain through for one hour. If you are reusing the pot from a previous year, thoroughly scrub it out before almost filling it with a layer of gritty planting medium.

2 Carefully remove the first echeveria from its pot and plant it in the container, taking care not to damage any flowers.

3 Repeat with the other plants for a full display. These plants were in full flower, and were perfectly happy to be transplanted in the summer, but it would be less damaging to do this in the spring before the flowers have appeared.

4 Mulch with a handful of gravel to keep the lower leaves off the soil, which could tend to rot them if damp.

AFTERCARE

Place on a windowsill with morning sun. Echeverias like a little shade in the afternoon. Water regularly in summer, if the weather is not too humid, but stop watering altogether during the winter months —or water monthly if brought indoors for the winter. Remove rotted leaves.

ABOVE: *Erigeron is a most satisfying no-fuss plant. Producing masses of flowers in summertime, it's hardy in most of the U.S. and perfectly happy in the near-drought conditions of the seaside. It'll be happy left to its own devices, but if you deadhead it regularly, you'll be rewarded with an even longer flowering period.*

boat garden

● *2 hours if planting from scratch; 30 minutes for annual revival*

Salty sea breezes offer a challenge to all but the most robust of plants, so for some guidance on easy-care gardening, you could do worse than take a walk along the coast. Look at what grows naturally, but also, for variety, take a peek into seaside front gardens. Because salt in the wind and soil make it difficult for most plants to take up and retain water, those that grow happily near the sea have developed ways to overcome this, in a similar way to any drought-resistant plants. You're likely to find grasses long and short swaying in the wind, the papery pompoms of thrift and statice (*Limonium*), and plants whose leaves are protected by essential oils, such as lavender, thyme, and rosemary. Create any garden with well-drained soil using a combination of these plants, and you shouldn't be too overburdened with day-to-day maintenance. This pretty little garden, planted in an old wooden boat, has graced the garden of a café on the south coast of England for several years. Each spring, the few plants that didn't survive the winter are dug out and replaced with new ones—then watering in the driest months is all this charming miniature garden demands.

you will need

A "retired" boat, if you can get one, or any large container painted gray-blue

Drill to make drainage holes

Broken-up polystyrene plant trays

Potting mix blended with 25 percent sharp sand and 25 percent gravel

Selection of seaside plants

1 If you're planting from scratch, make drainage holes in the bottom of the boat, then place a layer of broken-up polystyrene plant trays in the bottom. Next, add potting mix. If you're simply maintaining the boat garden, as here, dig out any plants that are past their best, line the bottom of the hole with potting mixture and plant in some lavender. Fill around the plant with the potting mix and press in firmly with your fingers.

2 Replenish another part of the boat with some delicately scented pinks (*Dianthus*) or perky pompom thrift (*Armeria*).

3 Finally, add in some grasses, making sure they're bedded into generous holes that have been lined with soil to help them withstand blustery winds. Thoroughly water in all the plants.

ABOVE: *The charm of this garden is that, instead of being packed with what could be over-flamboyant summer bedding, it celebrates the natural grassiness of the seaside, with splashes of color from pinks, lavender, and thrift. A drift of Erigeron daisies spills around one end of the boat like pink, frothy waves.*

AFTERCARE
Keep the plants well watered while they establish, then water during dry summer periods. Regularly deadhead the pinks to encourage repeat flowering. When the lavender flowers have dried out (usually around late summer or early fall), cut them down to the level of the leaves. Leave the thrift flowers to dry to a papery texture.

SOME FAVORITE SEASIDE FLOWERS
BELOW: *The delightful bobbing heads of thrift lend charm to any garden. The flowers appear in summer and gradually dry out to the papery texture of everlasting flowers. This white variety is called Armeria pseudarmeria 'Ballerina White'.*

Lavender, protected by natural oils, is excellent at surviving dry seasons and makes an excellent choice for seaside gardens, or for anyone who likes maintenance-free planting.

potted cattails

● *30 minutes*

If you love water plants but don't have the space or inclination to create a whole pond, plant some in a pot. They provide the ultimate form of easy-care gardening and could easily withstand a drought, even if you go on vacation for two weeks or more! Plant some pretty water lilies and floating plants in a pretty, decorative Chinese pot, or make a tall statement by planting lofty marginal water plants, such as cattails, striking striped horsetail (*Equisetum*), or elegant *Thalia* in a smooth-sided pot for a more Zen-like look.

These graceful plants are a smaller form of cattail. Tall and slim (around 2 ft/50 cm tall) with slender, pokerlike seed heads, they make a striking arrangement. They gently rustle in even the slightest breeze, providing an almost cinematic element in the garden, and look lovely positioned on the patio or as a focal point elsewhere in the garden.

ABOVE: *This cattail is tall and slender, with poker-like blooms.*

OPPOSITE: *Planted in a smooth-sided, watertight container, this elegant arrangement has a calming, Zen-like quality. It's a delightful way to bring a water garden element into even the smallest of gardens.*

you will need

Large, slatelike, fiberglass container with no drainage hole

Aquatic compost to fill the container up to a depth of 6 in (15 cm)

Pea gravel

Decorative pebbles

2 graceful cattail (*Typha laxmannii*) (zones 4–11)

1 Water plants are often sold in preplanted containers, which are simply lowered into ponds. This provides all the nutrients they need and stops them from becoming invasive. However, if you are planting in your own container, you might prefer to plant them directly into the aquatic compost so they can grow to fill out the pot.

3 Next, using a shovel or spade, cover the plastic with gravel to a thickness of about 2 in (5 cm).

4 Space the plants to check their positioning *in situ*, measuring the spacing if necessary. Allow about 18 in (45 cm) between the centers of each grass. Place a *Verbena bonariensis* (or other chosen flowering plant) between each grass.

5 Move the first pot to one side, and make a large cross cut in the plastic, making a hole about twice the size of the container.

6 Use large pebbles to hold back the cut plastic while you work, then use a spade to dig a large hole, twice the size of the grass root ball.

7 Line the bottom of the hole with potting mix. This will provide the plant with extra nutrients for lush growth while it becomes established.

8 Remove the plant from its pot, taking care not to cause any damage to the roots or disturb the root ball. Fill around the hole with more mix, pressing it down firmly with your fingers. Repeat with the other grasses and the verbenas (or other flowering plant). Once they are planted, water them all in well.

9 If you have any *Verbena bonariensis* that have self-seeded around the garden, tuck them in among the grasses for a good show next year.

AFTERCARE
Water the grasses regularly during the first year while they establish. After that, make sure they never dry out. Leave the grass "skeletons" in place over winter, but cut them back down to the ground in spring once you can see the new growth appearing. Cut the *Verbena bonariensis* to within 4 in (10 cm) of the ground in the fall once they have finished flowering.

10 Replace the cut-away plastic, tucking it in as close as possible to the roots of the grasses. Then, use a spade or rake to cover the area with gravel.

ivy heart

● *1 hour*

It will take you about an hour to make a simple topiary shape like this heart. After that, it will make a decorative feature that just keeps getting better, with little attention from you. Most English ivies will happily withstand the winter; as far north as zone 4. They're also happy in almost any position. Non-variegated cultivars, unlike most plants, positively love north-facing walls. Variegated ivies, such as this one, would also thrive in a north-facing spot, but you'd lose the pretty yellow element of its coloring.

you will need

Container

Galvanized garden wire

Masking tape

Potting mix

Long, trailing English ivy—about 6 individual roots (which might well be contained in a single pot from the garden center)

Bucket of water

OPPOSITE: *Heart-shaped topiary in a pretty variegated ivy makes a delightful focal point on the patio or in the garden. A heart is a simple shape to bend from wire, but for an even quicker and easier topiary, consider buying a ready-made shape to train the ivy up, such as a metal spiral.*

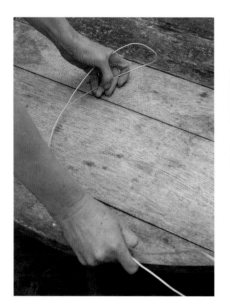

1 Start by making the heart shape. Cut a long piece of wire and bend it into a large circle, allowing for long "tails" of wire at each end that are equal to the depth of the container.

2 Make a dip in the circle opposite the tails, gradually bending the rest of the heart into shape. Make it your own: either taller and thinner, or a fuller heart shape, such as this.

3 Once you are happy with the shape, wrap masking tape firmly around the two tails to bind them together, making a firm foundation for the heart.

4 Fill the container with potting mix, then push the tails of the heart into the mix. Make any necessary adjustments to the heart shape.

5 If the pot of ivy you bought consists of several plants, gently tip it out, then plunge the whole thing into a bucket of water. This will release the soil from around the roots, making it easier for you to tease the individual plants apart without damaging them. Plant about six rooted ivies in the container around the wire heart, firmly bedding them into the potting mix.

6 Wind one ivy up one side of the wire heart shape and wind another up the other side, so they meet in the middle. Repeat with two more ivies on each side to thicken up the heart outline.

AFTERCARE

Keep watered. Do not allow to dry out. Add liquid feed once a month during the summer months to ensure good growth. If you overfeed variegated ivies, you may lose some of the color. As the ivy grows, prune back any extraneous offshoots to keep a clear heart shape.

OPPOSITE: *A pure white clematis entwines a cream-painted wooden column to provide instant structure in a deep border, making an excellent stand for a simple container planting of surfinia petunias.*

LEFT: *A striking and elegant calla lily is a marginal plant that likes to grow in shallow water. It's a great choice for a pond or bog garden.*

4 speedy structure

Striking structural elements are the secret of any interesting garden design. Without them, the space can seem a little formless; borders, amorphous. Structure can be introduced in many different ways by using different levels, pergolas, garden buildings, topiary, furniture groups, statuary, large pots, well defined and marked pathways . . . in fact, anything that brings a sculptural or architectural element to the garden. When it comes to "gardening in no time," this might seem a touch daunting. But it needn't be. Most people include a few containers in their gardens—and this is the simplest solution. Invest in the largest pot you can that is appropriate to the scale of your garden, and place it in a focal position, such as the center of a circular patio, then plant it with something dramatic. Box topiary used this way always makes a statement. Plant a pair for double the effect, placing them in a strategic place —either side of a path, for example.

Or think more laterally. Try trawling your local secondhand stores or garage sales for anything that might conceivably bring a structural element to the garden. An old chair, plant stand, pretty table, old cart . . . almost anything that offers structure will do. You might need to cheer it up with a lick of paint, but even that has unseen benefits. You could use the flowers in the border for color inspiration and paint the piece in a complementary hue, which would both intensify the tones of the planting at the height of the season and guarantee that the color remains all through the year. The other advantage of structure, even if it is of this more quirky kind, is that it can bring height to the garden, even when everything has died down in the winter, or in early spring before the plants reach full summer height.

take a chair

● *1 hour (make and plant about 1 pot per minute)*

A chair might not be the most obvious choice of structure to introduce to the garden, but it can work very well. Available in a wide variety of shapes and sizes, chairs have an architectural quality about them. They're also not difficult to find in secondhand stores or garage sales—or you could use one of your own if you have one that's broken or has fallen into disrepair. This commode might have seen better days, but it's an ideal candidate, as it has a ready-cut hole for you to fit the garden pot in. Dining chairs make good choices, too, because you can grow climbers up the legs and backs.

LEFT: *Clematis flowers, with their big, bold petals and vibrant color, add impact to any border.*

OPPOSITE: *This pretty basket chair was already painted pale purple when it was found in a secondhand store. The color went perfectly with the clematis in the* border, *while the woven texture has a natural feel that is simply perfect for a garden setting. All the chair needed was to be planted up with toning foxgloves and verbenas. Tucked into the flower bed close to the clematis, so that the flowers spill over the arm, it really looks as if it's always belonged here.*

you will need

Secondhand chair or commode

Garden pot to fit hole or shallow pot to put on the seat

1 foxglove (*Digitalis purpurea*) (zones 4–8)

1 *Verbena rigida*

1 million bells (Callibrachoa Million Bells Series)

Potting mix

Water-retaining gel

Slow-release fertilizer

1 Collect all the materials together. Thoroughly water all the plants and allow them to drain. This gives them a good start and helps them to establish themselves.

2 Place the garden pot in the commode hole. If you have an ordinary chair, you can either cut a hole using a jigsaw or choose a low terracotta dish in which to plant the plants.

3 Place a pebble or piece of crock over the drainage hole in the bottom of the pot, then using a trowel, put in a layer of potting mix.

4 Add slow-release fertilizer, following the manufacturer's instructions. This helps to support the plants throughout the growing season.

5 Now add some water-retaining gel, following the manufacturer's instructions, to reduce the chances of drying out during the summer months. Otherwise, during the hottest spells, the plants could need watering two or more times a day.

6 Carefully remove the foxglove from its pot without damaging its roots, and lower it into the chair pot.

OPPOSITE: *The lilac purple-painted chair lends emphasis to the purple flowers, providing a hint of color even when some of them are past their best.*

AFTERCARE

Keep the container well watered, and do not allow it to dry out. Once the foxglove finishes flowering, cut down the flower spike. Regularly deadhead the verbena and million bells. When the planting is past its best, you can remove the whole pot to another part of the garden for the dormant period or plant the foxglove and verbena into the ground. The foxglove should flower again for one more season. In early spring, cut down the brown leaves of the verbena: new shoots should appear for the next season's growth.

7 In the same way, remove the *Verbena rigida* from its pot and place it next to the foxglove. Considered an annual, it can be grown as a perennial in zones 8 and 9.

8 Finally, plant the million bells. Now fill any gaps with more potting mix, pressing it down firmly with your fingers. Thoroughly water the planting.

path finders

● *30 minutes*

One of the best ways to introduce structure to the garden is to use it to bring emphasis to features that are already there. This particularly applies to pathways (front and back), paved circles, and patio corners. One of the easiest ways to do this is to mark the feature with a pair of planters filled with (preferably) evergreen plants. You could choose architectural topiary balls, spirals, or cones, or a pair of elegant specimen plants, or go for something simpler, such as these pretty evergreen ferns in low-lead planters.

you will need

2 lead-effect planters
2 evergreen ferns, such as deer ferns (*Blechnum spicant*) (zones 5–8)
Gritty planting medium (made from roughly 50 percent soil-based potting mix, 25 percent sharp sand, and 25 percent gravel)

OPPOSITE: *A pair of ferns potted in lead-effect fiberglass containers marks the beginning of the path, emphasizing structure that already exists in the garden.*

ABOVE: *The pretty leaves of ferns make a classic choice for statement planting. Their feathery, vibrant green leaves combine strength with softness, taking on gentle rusty tones as they die back.*

1 Water the ferns and allow to drain. Thoroughly scrub out the containers, if necessary, then use a trowel to put a layer of at least 2 in (5 cm) of soil in the bottom.

2 Carefully remove the ferns from their plastic pots, retaining as much of their soil as possible.

3 Place the ferns in the containers. There are several varieties of evergreen ferns, but *Blechnum spicant* is particularly hardy and is readily available in both the United States and Europe.

OPPOSITE: *Ferns are found on every continent (except polar regions), and so can be used to create a timeless universal planting.*

4 Position the planted-up ferns to mark the end of a pathway, thereby emphasizing the structure in that part of the garden.

AFTERCARE

Ferns are best placed in a shady position, but some can tolerate a little sunshine. They need to be well watered and kept in moist, but not boggy, conditions. There is no need to add extra feed over the year.

classic column

● *Half a day (decorating the column); 1 hour (planting)*

Secondhand stores can often prove a fertile ground for structural ideas in the garden. This elegant, classical column was an unlikely find in an antique mirror shop! At the time, in plain wood it wasn't quite so elegant, but a coat of preservative paint soon changed that. It's a great height for any border, and can be placed in a gap or among lush planting to bring all-year structure. In winter, its creamy, classical lines lend interest to the emptier beds. Originally designed as an indoor plant stand, it can either be left as an unadorned pillar or used to provide a base for a succession of seasonal plantings.

LEFT: *There are plenty of white clematis varieties available, so choose the longest-flowering one from the garden center. You may also like to add another later-flowering one.*

OPPOSITE: *A cream-painted, classical column lends simple, elegant structure to the border. Clematis entwining itself up the column perfectly complements the carved flutes of the base and the acanthus-leaf detailing.*

you will need

Wooden column

Sandpaper

Paintbrush

Undercoat/primer formulated for outdoor use

Cream eggshell preservative paint formulated for outdoor use

Clematis **Mrs. George Jackman** (zones 4–8)

Clematis **Ice Blue** (zones 4–10)

Soft garden string

Shallow terracotta container

1 Surfinia Petunia 'yellow' (zones 5–9)

1 million bells (Callibrachoa Million Bells Series)

Potting mix

1 Lightly sand all the surfaces of the column, then paint with primer and undercoat. Allow to dry for a couple of hours or, better still, overnight.

2 Re-sand the column, then paint it using cream eggshell paint. Allow to dry overnight, or even longer to ensure that the paint is completely dried through.

3 Once the paint has completely dried and hardened, the column is ready to position in the border.

LEFT: *The column lends structure to the border, even in high summer, when the planting is lush and abundant. Use it to bring a bright element to the darker areas of the garden.*

4 Water all the plants and allow them to drain. Place the column in the border and dig a hole next to it. Place a layer of potting mix in the hole. Remove the supports from the potted clematis and tip it out of its pot. Place it in the hole and fill in with potting mix, pressing it down with your fingers.

5 Carefully disentangle the clematis stems to avoid breaking them. Then, using soft garden twine, loosely tie in the clematis at the base of the column.

6 Gently train the clematis up the column and tie it in place farther up the column. Thoroughly water the clematis.

7 Place a layer of potting mix in the bottom of the terracotta container, add the Surfinia petunias and Million Bells, and fill around and between them with more potting mix. Thoroughly water, then position the container on top of the column.

AFTERCARE
Clematis likes to be in full sun with its roots in the shade. Water regularly. Check the variety of clematis for when and how much to prune. Water the container regularly, and deadhead all the flowers to encourage repeat flowering throughout the season.

the great divide

● *2 hours*

Using trellis to divide off sections of the garden is a classic way of creating structure. Paint the trellis for garden color, then plant pretty climbers to make a delightful growing screen. This trellis was already *in situ* near the end of the garden, providing a screen for a plant nursery section behind. But it was not a glorious sight, set in scrubby land that was difficult to plant. The solution was to plant climbers, which would prettily clamber over the trellis, lending delightful structure to the end of the garden

you will need

2 large terracotta pots
Potting mix
1 *Clematis* 'Elsa Späth' (zones 4–11)
1 *Clematis* **Anna Louise** (zones 4–9)
1 star jasmine (*Trachelospermum jasminoides*) (zones 7–10)
Large pebbles or cobbles for mulch
Soft garden twine
Bags of 2-in (5-cm) blue slate chips

ABOVE: *Beautiful blue* Clematis **Anna Louise**, *with its feathery white center, blooms all through the summer and makes an ideal choice for training over trellis.*

OPPOSITE: *A deep violet clematis teams delightfully with the pale green-blue trellis and is complemented by evergreen star jasmine (*Trachelospermum jasminoides*) in the pot behind. This provides the combination of all-year cover with the glorious clematis hues during the summer. This photograph was taken about two months after planting.*

1 Gather all the materials together before starting, water all the plants well, and allow to drain.

2 Plant the clematis in one container, making sure that the root ball is 3–6 in (7–15 cm) below the surface. This promotes growth and protects against clematis wilt disease. Water the plant well.

3 Mulch the surface with pebbles or cobbles. This is important for clematis, because although they thrive in plenty of sun, they like to keep their roots in shade.

4 Train the clematis up the trellis, tying it in using soft garden string, which will not do any damage to the plants.

5 Plant the star jasmine in the second container, training it up the trellis and tying it in. It is important this plant be planted in as large a pot as possible, as it likes plenty of moisture until it is established.

OPPOSITE: *Star jasmine (also called Confederate jasmine) is a brilliant choice for growing up trellis: evergreen, its leaves turn a rich bronze in winter. It produces pretty white flowers from mid- to late summer.*

6 Empty the blue slate pieces around the area to create an attractive mulch.

7 Although the plants don't even begin to cover the trellis when first planted, by midsummer they will already have made good progress—as illustrated on page 110.

AFTERCARE

Keep all the plants well watered in the first year while they establish themselves. In subsequent years, the star jasmine, in particular, becomes very drought tolerant. As both plants grow, tie in the new shoots. Lightly prune the clematis in spring – but both 'Elsa Späth' and **Anna Louise** have flowerbuds on old wood (they are group 2), so take care not to cut off the buds in spring. The main prune of the clematis is after flowering in early summer. Thin out or prune the star jasmine as needed.

wheelbarrow bog garden

● *1 hour*

Unless you have a particularly boggy area in your garden, creating a bog area can have its problems—not least of which is keeping the place moist. Yet there are some fabulous bog plants. If you'd like to grow some, one option is to plant them in a wheelbarrow. It serves as a good-sized container that adds structure to the garden; and, with no drainage holes, it will keep the soil suitably damp. This one has been "parked" at the edge of some decking, bringing interest to an area that couldn't otherwise be planted.

LEFT: *Giant gunnera is a plant that definitely makes a statement! Its crinkly, deep-veined leaves add texture and look spectacular when the sun shines through them, as here.*

you will need

Old wheelbarrow

Garden soil

Giant gunnera or prickly rhubarb (*Gunnera manicata*) (zones 6–8)

Spotted calla lily *(Zantedeschia albomaculata)* (zones 7–11)

Pebbles or cobbles for mulch

OPPOSITE: *Calla lilies make a fabulous sight; but, being bog plants, they need plenty of moisture. The giant gunnera is another spectacular plant whose leaves can grow up to 6 ft (2 m) across. It's unlikely to grow to that extent within the limits of the wheelbarrow—though it may need to be replaced in a few years' time by a younger plant if it outgrows its space.*

1 Thoroughly water the plants. Using a spade, fill the wheelbarrow to within about 6 in (15 cm) of the rim with garden soil.

2 Dig a shallow hole in the garden soil to accommodate the giant gunnera, so that the root ball is about 2 in (5 cm) below the top of the wheelbarrow.

3 Carefully remove the calla lily from its pot and position it in the wheelbarrow in the same way as the gunnera. Fill around both plants with garden soil to about 2 in (5 cm) of the rim of the wheelbarrow, pressing it in firmly with your fingers.

4 Use pebbles and/or cobbles to completely cover the surface of the soil. This not only looks good: it also serves as a mulch to help retain the moisture.

OPPOSITE: *The exquisite, white-spotted calla lily, also known as arum lily and lily of the Nile, adds an elegant appearance to the bog garden.*

5 Thoroughly water in all the plants, making sure the soil is completely dampened.

AFTERCARE

Keep moist at all times. The gunnera leaves will die back in the fall. Cut them off and use them to cover the crown of the plant to protect it from frost. Because both plants are hardy only in warm zones, it's advisable, in cooler zones, to wheel the barrow into a toolshed or greenhouse during the winter. The calla lily is semi-evergreen, but evergreen in hot regions.

ABOVE: *Pebbles strung on garden wire make a natural-looking—and weatherproof!—garden "picture".*

fireplace feature

● *1 hour 30 minutes*

You can use architectural salvage to create structure in the garden. This fireplace was in the courtyard of a disused pottery. But there's nothing to stop you putting an old mantelpiece in your own garden as a frame for plants and containers. Hang a mirror above it, it you like, to reflect light and lush borders back into the garden. Either use a damaged fireplace that has been replaced or rummage around in architectural salvage yards. Old windows, radiators, cupboards, and shelves make ingenious alternatives.

you will need

Pebbles with holes in, collected from the beach
Heavy-gauge garden wire
Wooden picture frame, painted white
Hook, masonry drill, and wall anchor
2 grapevines (*Vitis vinifera*) (zones 6–8)
2 thrift (*Armeria* 'Ballerina White') (zones 6–8)
3 lavender (*Lavandula angustifolia*) (zones 5–8)
1 *Echeveria* or other compact potted plant
6 terracotta pots (2 large, 4 small)
Potting mix

OPPOSITE: *Make a feature of a damaged or disused fireplace by wittily treating it as if it were inside. Hang a pebble "picture" above it, then train a couple of grapevines over it. Here, potted plants fill the void of the fireplace.*

1 Thread pebbles with holes in them onto a heavy-gauge wire, finishing the end by bending it into a hook. Bend into a spiral.

2 Fix a hook to the wall above the mantel, using a masonry drill and wall anchor, as appropriate. Hang the pebble spiral on the hook and the picture frame around it.

3 Plant each grapevine in a large terracotta pot, with a thrift in front, and the lavender in smaller pots, and arrange them around the fireplace. Plant the *Echeveria* in a small terracotta pot and place on the mantel.

put in a pond

● *1 day (if digging out pond); 3 hours (if planting an existing pond)*

Ponds make a delightful feature , reflecting the light of the water and offering an environment for different plants and animals. There are many kinds of pond liner available, from flexible polyethylene to rigid, preformed fiberglass liners. The preformed kind are the easiest to install, though this is not the quickest of projects. However, once the hole has been dug and the pond liner installed, the pond itself can be planted very quickly indeed.

you will need

Installed pond liner
Flat stone slabs to cover the top edge
Mortar (and pebbles, if desired)
1 water lily (*Nymphaea* 'Marliacea Chromatella') (zones 5–10)
2 narrow-leaved reedmace (*Typha angustifolia*) (zones 3–10)
2 pickerel weed (*Pontederia cordata*) (zones 3–9)
1 *Sisyrinchium californicum* (zones 9–11)
5 bunches of oxygenating plants per 10.75 square foot (1 square metre)

OPPOSITE: *Even a tiny pond brings an extra dimension to the garden. The liner of this one was put in and planted in July. A month later, when this photograph was taken, it had filled out considerably to create this delightful feature at the bottom of the garden.*

ABOVE: *Their sculptural flowers opening out in the sunshine, water lilies make a delightful focus for any pond. Moreover, their large, floating leaves serve as a landing platform for tiny frogs, newly developed from tadpoles.*

1 Follow the manufacturer's instructions to fit and fill the preformed liner. These come ready-made, with different levels for planting. To fit them, you need to excavate a hole to accommodate the liner, then add a protective layer of builder's sand as underlay before putting the liner in.

2 Use the flat stone slabs to cover the edge of the pond, arranging them to make a pleasing edging. Once the slabs are arranged, fix them in place using a mortar mixture. If desired, also fill in the gaps between the stone slabs with pebbles.

3 Lower the lily into the deepest part of the pond. Water lilies are often sold preplanted in baskets, so that all you need to do is position the basket then remove the handles.

4 Now lower the basket of narrow-leaved reedmace into the shallow end of the pond. Make sure not to buy cat's tail (*Typha latifolia*), which is far too invasive for small garden ponds.

5 Next, install the pickerel weed on a shallow shelf. This may not look very exciting when you plant it, but once it's mature, it will produce flower spikes of a vibrant blue.

OPPOSITE: *This round pond, planted mainly with water lilies and overhung by Cyanara cardunculus (artichoke), is a simple alternative to the free-form shape used in the main project.*

6 Finally, add the *Sisyrinchium* on a shallow shelf. This wonderful, structural plant, much like a miniature iris, produces pretty, pale yellow flowers. However, it is not very hardy; so if you live in zone 8 or colder you may wish to find an alternative at your garden center. You will also need to put in some submerged oxygenating plants to help retain a healthy balance in the pond.

AFTERCARE
During the summer, keep the pond filled with water. If any carpet-forming floating plants appear, control them by netting them off and discarding them. If algae appear, remove them either with a cane with a nail on the end, or by hand. Cut down any plants that die off in the winter.

plant theater

● *1 hour*

There was a great Victorian tradition of creating plant "theaters", in which plants, often of a single species, were arranged on staging as a focal point in the garden. Even if nowadays we're less inclined to be so studied, the idea is a good one, and we can interpret it in our own ways. Search out any interesting piece that can be used to display plants, then gather together a group of plants that work well together, and you have an instant structure to bring impact to the garden.

you will need

Metal cart

Selection of enamel and terracotta containers with drainage holes

Selection of drought-resistant plants, including houseleeks (*Sempervivum*), echeverias, sedums, small euphorbias such as *E. myrsinites*

2 zucchini plants

OPPOSITE: *This green-painted, vintage metal cart makes an ideal plant "theater", providing a platform for a collection of yellow-flowered plants in enamel and terracotta containers. Overall, it creates impact in the corner of a pebble garden.*

RIGHT: *No cart? No problem! Use the planting-in-cans idea, but simply group them on a table to make a pretty still life.*

1 Start by placing the zucchini plants, planted in enamel dishes, at diagonally opposite ends of the cart to begin to create a pleasing display.

2 Place a yellow-flowering sedum, such as *Sedum kamischaticum* var. *floriferum* 'Weihenstephaner Gold', on the bottom shelf of the cart.

3 Plant houseleeks in an enamel colander and an *Echeveria* in a terracotta pot and add to the middle shelf. Add a yellow-flowering sedum. On the top shelf, add *Sedum spurium* and a small euphorbia planted in an enamel pitcher.

OPPOSITE: *You don't need to set aside a whole vegetable bed in the garden. Follow the example of traditional potager gardens, where flowers and produce happily grow together in the borders.*

LEFT: *If you don't have a greenhouse, raise the seedlings under bell jars. They're not only practical; they also make a decorative feature in the spring and early summer.*

5 grow your own

There's something magical about growing your own meals from tiny seeds over the course of a few months. In return for a little effort, by the end of the summer, you could be sinking your teeth into your very own sun-ripened tomatoes, exploding with a flavor that could never be replicated by its harvested-when-still-green supermarket cousin. Or your kitchen might be filled with the fragrant perfume of fully ripe, picked-that-morning strawberries; your colander overflowing with fresh beans.

We normally think of growing food as something that requires large amounts of space, dedication, and professional know-how. But you don't have to be a farmer to make a stab at growing your own. You can allocate one bed in the flower garden, grow edibles among the flowers, or simply confine your vegetable plot to a patio or windowsill. So long as you have room for a plant pot or a grow bag, you have space to grow some food.

If you want to grow from seed, you need to start thinking as early as March about what you'd like, so you have time to buy the seeds and start them off in April, because the fruits and vegetables need to be advanced enough by midsummer to have time to ripen fully before the cold weather. Timings will vary from one region to another, so check with a garden center. Over the next few pages, we help you get the seeds started and offer space-saving growing ideas. For the finer details on how to cultivate the seeds you decide to grow, follow the instructions on the seed packets. We've chosen easy-to-grow produce that we've found offers plenty to harvest, such as tomatoes, runner beans, and zucchini.

paper seed pots

● *5 minutes to make and plant 1 pot*

There's something deeply satisfying about making these little pots for your seeds. It's a great way to recycle old newspapers; and when the plants are ready to be put into the ground, you just plant the whole ensemble, pot and all, into its final growing spot. As you harvest the beans, tomatoes, and zucchini and you remember the improbably small seeds that you tipped out of a paper envelope, you feel like the cleverest, most creative person in the world. Of course, we all know it was Mother Nature that really did the work —but those seeds did need the right environment and a little tender loving care from you. Starting them off in their seed trays appeals to one's deepest sense of order, and there are many ways you can satisfy this while giving your seedlings the best start.

LEFT: *Making paper pots is simplicity itself using a wooden potter, and once made, they're surprisingly resilient.*

OPPOSITE: *Newspaper pots provide a practical solution to raising seedlings: they're bio-degradable, so the seedlings can be planted straight into the ground, pot and all, avoiding any damage to the roots. They also look very cute, especially lined up in an attractive container.*

you will need

Scissors
Newspaper
Wooden potter
Seed-starting mix
Seeds of your choice

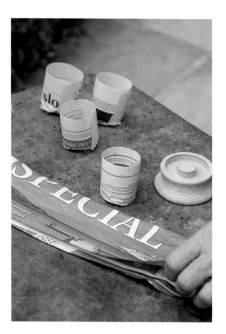

1 Using a large pair of scissors, cut strips of newspaper about 3 x 22 in (8 x 57 cm) —one strip makes one pot.

2 Roll one newspaper strip loosely around the main body of the potter.

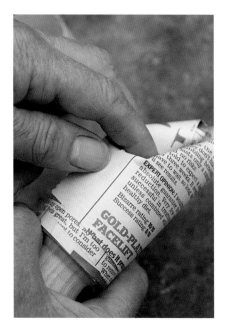

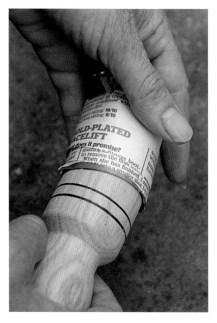

3 When the whole strip has been rolled up, use your fingers to fold in the excess paper—first one side, and then the other.

4 Now press the main body of the potter into the base and twist it to seal the pot.

5 Gently slip the pot off the potter. You'll find this much easier to do if the paper was wound loosely around the potter.

6 When all the pots have been made, fill them with seed-starting mix, pressing it in lightly with your thumb, so that it is firm but not too tightly packed.

7 Line the pots up into a seed tray or other container and plant one seed into each pot.

8 Gently water all the planted pots.

AFTERCARE

Keep the seedlings watered and protect from frost under glass. They can be planted straight into the ground once they are large enough and there's no danger of frost.

peat pellets

● *15 minutes*

Another, super-simple way to start seeds off is by inserting them in special compressed pellets, or plugs, made of peat (or sometimes of coir), which are available online and from some garden centers. The pellets, or plugs, which are contained in a biodegradable covering, give the seeds the best possible chance of germinating. The specially adapted seed tray keeps the pellets in place and prevents overwatering, while the domed lid maintains warmth and humidity, giving the seedlings the best start in life. Best of all, when the seedlings are big enough, you can transfer them, plug and all, into a larger pot or straight into the ground, without disturbing the roots; there they can grow on to maturity.

ABOVE: *The neatly compressed pellets look like large coins, but once they are watered, they increase to about four times their original size.*

1 The pellets are ready installed in the trays, though they can slip, so check they are all in their correct position.

2 Add warm water to the tray: within a few minutes, the pellets will expand to about 1 in (2.5 cm) tall.

3 Fluff up the peat surface and plant one large seed or two or three smaller ones in each pellet.

ABOVE: *Young plants need to be brought on under glass until they're strong enough to go into the ground. If you're short of space, it's lovely to make even the plantlet stage beautiful, so plant them in pretty little enamel containers and enjoy their nursery stage!*

bell-jar beauty

● *15 minutes*

If you don't have a greenhouse but would still like to grow your own vegetables, take a tip from the Victorians and protect your plantlets under a bell jar. It not only behaves like a mini-greenhouse, protecting the young plants from frost, but also creates a microclimate whereby the moisture given off by the plants condenses within the jar, creating a self-watering system. The bell jar also protects the plants from damage by pests. Start raising the seeds in seed trays, paper pots, or peat pellets. When they're strong enough, pot them on, keeping them protected under the bell jar until the threat of frost

you will need

2 bell jars	Hammer
2 small enamel containers	Seed-starting or potting mix
Masking tape	A large pot or bucket
Gimlet or other sharp tool	1 young plant per bell jar (these are vegetable marrows)

1 First, make holes in the enamel containers. Start by placing a piece of masking tape in the bottom of each container. This is to prevent your hole-piercing tool from slipping as you make the hole. Now, using a gimlet or other sharp implement and a hammer, make a hole in the bottom of the container.

2 Thoroughly water the plants and allow to drain. Place a layer of soil in the bottom of the container. Place the plant in the container and add more soil around it, pressing it in firmly with your fingers until the plant is fully bedded in. Thoroughly water in.

OPPOSITE: *If you don't want to keep the plantlets inside, cover them with bell jars so you can put them straight outside. The bell jars are not only practical—they're beautiful, too, bringing interest to the garden early in the year. They're the perfect solution for smaller plots that have neither space for a greenhouse nor large vegetable patches. You can raise the young plants under the domes; then, if you're really short of space, plant them out in the borders among the flowers.*

AFTERCARE

Keep the seedlings well watered. Once they are strong enough and there's no risk of frost, plant them outside in the ground.

micro vegetable patch

● *1 hour 30 minutes*

If you haven't got space for a vegetable garden, you can still grow your own vegetables using a grow bag. Most of these are made of plain black polypropylene and are relatively inconspicuous, but they're not terribly attractive either. You can conceal the bag using basketwork hurdles, as shown here for a low rectangular bag, or, if the bag is round or square you could simply place it in a large basket. If the bag is vividly colored, you can conceal the top with some coconut matting. Position the bag in a sunny spot.

you will need

Grow bag plus potting compost if needed

4 hurdle sections, 8 plastic ties, and coconut matting (optional) cut to fit

Scissors

2 tomato plants

1 basil plant

1 nasturtium plant

2 bamboo canes

2 cane toppers

LEFT AND OPPOSITE: *Grow yourself a basil and tomato salad that will last all summer. Given a grow bag and hurdles or basket, you can grow produce in the smallest spaces. The coconut matting provides* *mulch to prevent weed growth, so your little vegetable plot will require only the minimum of attention. Very soon, the plants will grow to cover it, adding up to a charming miniplot.*

1 Collect all the materials together and thoroughly water all the plants, then leave them to drain while you put the hurdles together.

2 Use the plastic ties to join the pieces together. At each corner, use one tie at the top and one at the bottom of the hurdle pieces.

3 Puncture the bottom of the grow bag to make drainage holes, if necessary. A black polypropylene bag will need to be filled with potting mix. Place the filled bag inside the hurdles or basket.

4 If using coconut matting, place this over the bag. Position the plants on top to check the spacing, then cut through both plastic and matting as shown.

5 Use your hands to create a space in the soil. Remove each plant from and insert it as shown; for open-topped grow bags, dig a small hole with a trowel and plant as usual. Water the plants thoroughly. Position a cane next to each plant and tie the plant to it. Place a small plant pot on each cane as a safety topper, to protect your eyes.

AFTERCARE

Keep the plants watered. To encourage a strong single stem, snap out the sideshoots that grow in the tomato leaf joints. When the tomatoes have produced four trusses, pinch out the growing tip to encourage the plant to put its energy into producing healthy fruit. Water daily and feed with tomato fertilizer weekly. Remove dead leaves. Once the tomatoes are full-size, remove most of the leaves to expose the fruit to the sun. Pinch out any basil flowers so that the plant puts its energy into producing the leaves. The nasturtiums will deter blackfly. Deadhead to encourage repeat flowering.

raised vegetable plot

● *30 minutes*

Traditionally, there are two reasons for planting vegetables. First, it reduces the risk of back strain for the gardener; second, once summer is here and the air is warm, having the plants above ground level warms the soil they're growing in and speeds their development. If you don't have a large plot, one of the simplest solutions is to plant your vegetables in a crate, which is both economical of space and transportable, so it can be moved to a sunny spot where it will thrive.

you will need

Old wooden fruit box or crate
Sheet of plastic or black trash bag
Scissors
Potting mix
Soil sieve
Sweetcorn seed

FAR LEFT AND OPPOSITE: *An old fruit box is a perfect container for a miniature raised bed. It's robust and manageable, and looks appropriately rural.*

1 Cut the black plastic more or less to the size of the bottom of the crate, then cut holes into it for drainage. Lay the plastic in the bottom of the crate.

2 Sift potting mix into the crate, filling it to within 1 in (2.5 cm) of the top of the crate.

3 Use a dibble to make 1-in (2.5-cm) holes and plant the seeds about 12 in (30 cm) apart. Water well and cover. Protect the crate with burlap or newspaper, until the threat of frost is over.

AFTERCARE

Keep the soil well watered and weed free. The sweetcorn will grow over the summer and will be ready to harvest when the silky tassels at the tops of the cobs turn brown, Check their progress by carefully peeling back the leaves.

bright and beautiful

● *1 hour*

If you lack space but would love to grow vegetables, plant some in inexpensive, vibrant containers. They are easily movable and could even take up residence on a balcony. This combination consists of runner beans, tomatoes, and zucchini, all chosen because they yield generous crops in a small space. Nasturtiums have been added for their pretty leaves and to bring extra color through the summer. When they produce seeds, late in the summer, these can be added to salads. Another advantage is that, although blackfly are attracted to runner beans, they prefer nasturtiums, so are more likely to leave the beans alone. If blackfly do arrive, squash them on the stalks with your fingers. They will keep coming over the course of a few days, so do this every day for a week. If they do take up residence, spray them off with the hose using the jet spray. The final resort would be to spray with insecticide suitable for fruit and vegetables.

you will need

3 colorful plastic or rubber flexible buckets
Corkscrew
Potting mix
1 zucchini 'Ambassador' F1
2 plum tomato plants, such as *Lycopersicon lycopersicum* 'Bush Celebrity'
3 dwarf runner bean 'Hestia'
9 trailing nasturtiums (*Tropaeolum* spp.)
Thin wooden poles or bamboo cones
Soft garden string
Liquid feed

ABOVE AND OPPOSITE: *Colorful and inexpensive tub trugs make excellent containers for a movable mini vegetable garden. Add nasturtiums to the plantings to add color and to keep the blackfly off the beans.*

1 Thoroughly water all the plants and allow them to drain. Turn the buckets upside-down and make 4–6 holes in the bottom of each one, using a corkscrew.

2 Half-fill the buckets with soil.

3 Remove the zucchini from its pot, taking care not to damage its roots, then plant it in the center of one of the buckets. Firm the soil around the plant, using your fingers.

4 Add three nasturtiums, placing them evenly around the zucchini. Fill with soil and press in well with your fingers.

5 In the same way, plant up another bucket with the two tomato plants. Plum tomatoes are a good choice, because they produce delicious, firm fruit that is not too heavy for the vine.

6 In the same way, plant up the dwarf runner beans in the third bucket. Place the plant in the center of the container, then fill around with soil to about 1 in (2.5 cm) from the top. Firm in with your fingers.

7 Cut the poles or bamboo canes to length. The tomatoes will need about 4 ft (1.2 m) to allow them to be pushed into the soil at the bottom of the container. For the beans, check the plant label for the finished height.

8 Use at least one pole, or bamboo cane to support each tomato and bean plant. To give even more support, make a simple "teepee" of canes.

9 Tie each of the plants to a pole, using soft garden twine. This will not damage the young shoots. Do not use garden wire, as it is likely to cut into the stems and damage them as they grow.

10 Tie all the canes in each tub trug together near the tops, then wrap the string around the stems several times for extra strength and tie the ends in a square knot, which won't slip.

11 Make up a solution of liquid feed, following the manufacturer's instructions. First fill the watering can to capacity. Then measure in the correct amount of feed to make the solution to the correct strength.

12 Thoroughly water the containers using the liquid feed solution. This will help to settle the soil into any air spaces, while giving the plants the best start.

AFTERCARE

Place the containers in a sunny position and keep them all well watered. Feed weekly throughout the summer until all fruits have been harvested.

Tomatoes

Pinch out the sideshoots. Once 6–7 trusses have formed, pinch out the top. Harvest as soon as they ripen.

Runner beans

Pinch out the tops once they reach the top of the poles. Harvest the beans while they are young and tender to encourage the growth of new beans.

Zucchini

The zucchini can be allowed to grow over the edge of the container, but you can also tie it to a stake as it grows. Harvest fruits when they are young.

great companions

● *30 minutes*

When your space is limited to just one vegetable plant in a pot, such as a tomato, you need it to work well and to be productive. One way to protect it against pests is to take the age-old principles of companion planting and put different plants together in a container. Vegetable gardeners have traditionally planted French marigolds in tomato beds to deter both blackfly and whitefly. French marigolds also exude a substance from their roots that kills parasitic nematodes. But that aside, the marigolds, with their vibrant, burnished tones, bring color to the container while the plants are growing and the green fruits are developing.

LEFT AND OPPOSITE: *There's something very straightforward about tomatoes, so no need to fuss with them. Just plant them in a simple terracotta pot with French marigolds for color and for protection against blackfly and whitefly.*

you will need

Terracotta pot

Potting mix

1 tomato plant

6 double marigold (*Tagetes patula* sp. 'Marmalade')

Liquid tomato feed

Bamboo cane

Raffia or soft garden string

1 Collect all the materials together and thoroughly water all the plants and let them drain. Scrub out the container, making sure it is completely clean. Place a piece of crock over the drainage hole to prevent the soil from seeping out.

2 Using a trowel, fill the container three quarters full with soil. Use potting mix because this is specially formulated and has already been treated with extra fertilizers to give the plants a good strong start.

3 Remove the tomato plant from its pot, taking care not to damage the roots. This is particularly important if you are planting a more mature plant, as its roots will be more developed than those of a seedling. Place the plant in the center of the container.

4 In the same way, remove the marigolds from their pots and arrange them around the tomato. Fill around and between the plants with soil and press it in firmly with your fingers.

5 Place the bamboo cane in the soil near the tomato, pushing it to the bottom of the container. Using raffia or soft garden string, tie the main stem to the bamboo in several places up its length for support. Trim the ends using scissors.

AFTERCARE

Tomato
Pinch out the new sideshoots to encourage upward growth. Once four trusses have formed, pinch out the leading shoot so the plant puts its energy into developing the fruit. Water daily. Feed with liquid tomato feed every two weeks. Remove any dead leaves. Once the fruits are full-size, remove any other leaves to allow full sun on the fruits to ripen them.
Marigolds
Keep the marigolds watered. Deadhead regularly to encourage repeat flowering.

potager pretty

● *2 hours 30 minutes*

Vegetable gardens can be pretty as well as practical. Take a leaf from the traditional *potager*, the French term for an ornamental kitchen garden that combines produce with herbs and cutting flowers. So whether you intersperse vegetables among the main borders or reserve a "mainly vegetable" area and embellish it with seasonal flowers, you can have your garden and eat it! Either plant everything together at the beginning of the season or—if, as here, you feel the vegetable garden could do with a little extra colour—add some flowers later in the season.

you will need

2 foxgloves (*Digitalis purpurea* 'Dalmatian Purple') (zones 5–9)

3 *Scabiosa atropurpurea* (zones 9–11)

12 *Verbena* plants of three or four species/cultivars (typically zones 6–9), such as V. 'Homestead Purple' and V. *rigida*

Potting mix

OPPOSITE, RIGHT: *Purples work well together, especially when you team the whole range from the purple-blue of the scabious to the magenta of Verbena 'Claret', and will brighten the vegetable patch right up to the end of September and beyond.*

ABOVE: *By mid-July, the vegetable bed had grown up, but there were still large patches of empty ground with very little color, which could be cheered up with some seasonal flowers.*

1 Gather all the plants together, thoroughly water them, and let them drain. Position the plants, still in their pots, in the border between the vegetables.

2 Put one potted plant to one side as you dig a hole in the position you want to plant it. Make the hole twice the size of the pot.

3 Line the hole with potting mix. Do this by putting a 2-in (5-cm) layer at the bottom before positioning the plant.

4 Place the plant in the hole and fill
  around it with potting mix, pressing it in
firmly with your fingers.

5 Once all the plants are planted and
  firmed in, give them a good watering.

AFTERCARE
Keep all the plants well watered throughout
the summer and deadhead the scabious and
verbenas regularly in order to encourage
repeat flowering.

OPPOSITE: *Pile on the color impact of red hot chilies by planting them in a bright blue container and underplanting with vibrant Celosia, making an arrangement pretty enough for the flower garden, even before the chilies begin to show color.*

LEFT: *Strawberries usually grow on the ground, but you can enjoy their fruit and make a spectacular display by planting them in a reproduction Victorian hanging basket and supplementing them with vibrant red verbenas.*

6 delicious and decorative

Vegetable patches display a wonderful sense of order: serried ranks of uniform plants filling beds in a living graphic display. But many of us do not have the space for vegetable patches, and frankly, although they look lush and gorgeous in early summer, as the season progresses, they can be a touch untidy. Also, bred for their fruits, leaves, or roots, edible plants don't necessarily look beautiful in themselves. The solution, if you want to grow food in your flower garden, is to introduce decorative elements. Choose witty containers, add pretty decoration, come up with colorful solutions for supports and protection against destructive wildlife. With these ideas in place, your food plants will mix happily with the more decorative elements of your garden planting.

Another key is to introduce color, since food plants often have insignificant flowers (apologies to zucchini, which regularly produce fabulous, orange-yellow blooms). You can do this by using paint on pots, supports, nearby fences or trellis, which will bring all-year color whether the plants are in leaf, bloom, or fruit . . . and even in the winter, when everything's died down. Choose a paint that is complementary to the plant—so it might echo the flower or fruit color, or complement the leaves.

Alternatively, bring color and interest to growing produce by placing plants with long flowering seasons next to them. This works especially well if the blooms complement the colors of the fruit. The next few pages are filled with ideas to get you started. Use them for inspiration, then come up with some original ones for yourself.

herb rack

● *1 hour 30 minutes*

Plant your favorite herbs in pretty pastel, enamel buckets to create the freshest of herb racks to hang outside the kitchen door, just where you need them. They'll grow throughout the summer, ensuring a continuous fresh supply. Choose plants to suit your family's needs—if you need huge handfuls every day, start out with larger plants, so they have time to put on more growth before you've stripped them bare. One of these buckets has been filled with nasturtiums. Their pretty, rounded leaves, at the ends of wiggly stems, add charm to the arrangement from the outset. Later, their red and yellow flowers will bring vibrancy and, eventually, their seeds can be used to add a lively, peppery flavor to salads.

you will need

6 small enamel buckets
Hammer, bradawl or gimlet to make holes
Potting mix
Water-retaining gel
Slow-release plant fertilizer
Selection of herbs of your choice
Green garden string

LEFT AND OPPOSITE: *Pretty, little, green enamel buckets lend structure and color to the arrangement. You can hang them on hooks or wires (as here) or arrange them on garden shelves like a plant theater (see page 125).*

1 Thoroughly water all the herbs and allow them to drain.

2 Meanwhile, make drainage holes in the bottoms of the buckets, using a hammer and a sharp instrument such as a bradawl or gimlet.

3 Put a handful of potting mix into the bottom of each bucket.

4 Add water-retaining gel, following the manufacturer's instructions. Repeat with the slow-release plant feed. Thoroughly mix the water-retaining gel and plant feed into the soil.

5 Remove the first herb, here a thyme, from its pot and plant it in one of the buckets.

6 Fill the edges with soil and press in firmly with your fingers.

7 Repeat with herbs such as chives, marjoram, and nasturtiums.

8 Repeat with Eau-de-Cologne mint (this one is *Mentha × piperita f. citrata*).

9 Use green garden string to hang up the buckets. These have been hung on galvanized wires used to train red currants. Alternatively, you could hang them from a tree or even from cup hooks fixed into a piece of driftwood. Thoroughly water the finished arrangement.

RIGHT: *Thyme produces pretty little flowers early in the summer. Although they provide a decorative element to the display, it's best to remove them to encourage the plant to concentrate on producing the aromatic essential oils, rather than flowers and seeds.*

AFTERCARE

Keep watered throughout the summer. Cut as needed but, in the early weeks, take care not to denude the plants; otherwise they will die back. Once they're properly established, they should put on rapid growth through the summer.

tasty lessons

● *1 hour*

With their wildflower looks and heady fragrance, a collection of herbs in a container makes for an irresistible summer arrangement. The fact that home-grown herbs bring so much fresh flavor to summer cooking is almost a bonus. But although they look fresh and pretty when young, as they grow, herbs can look, well . . . messy. So the trick, when putting them together, is to choose varieties with very different leaves. This planting combines grasslike chives, tied up to keep them under control; a pretty strawberry plant; lush, variegated pineapple mint; delicate, flat-leaved parsley; and feathery dill.

OPPOSITE: *The interior of an old school desk makes a delightful herb bed, which can be placed exactly where you need it. Preferably position it in a sunny spot.*

you will need

Old school desk or hall table with a drawer
Drill or bradawl
Black-plastic trash bag
Scissors
Potting mix
String
3 chive plants (zones 4–10)
1 dill (zones 8–10)
1 strawberry plant (zones 4–8)
1 pineapple mint (zones 6–11)
1 flat-leaved parsley (zones 6–9)
Slow-release plant fertilizer
Pebbles for mulch

1 Water all the plants and allow them to drain. Make drainage holes in the bottom of the desk. If you are using a hall table with a drawer, use a jigsaw to cut the top off the table and make drainage holes in the bottom of the drawer. Cut the black plastic to line the desk or drawer, then cut holes in it for drainage.

2 Using a trowel, carefully half-fill the desk with potting mix, which comes ready-formulated with fertilizers to give the plants a good, strong start.

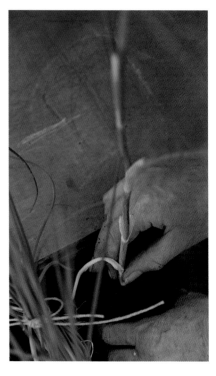

3 Use string to tie the chives loosely into neat bundles, then knock them out of their pots.

4 Place the chives in a line along one short end of the desk.

5 Add the dill next to the chive plant at the back of the desk.

6 Carefully take the strawberry plant from its pot and place it in the front right-hand corner of the desk.

7 In the same way, remove the pineapple mint from its pot and place it behind the strawberry at the back of the desk.

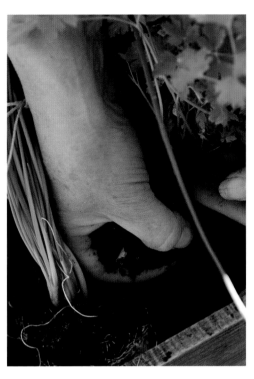

8 Place the flat-leaved parsley at the front, in-between the strawberry and the chives.

9 Fill between and around the herbs with soil and press down firmly with your fingers.

10 Carefully place pebbles on top of the soil. They look pretty and help to retain moisture.

11 Strawberry runners can be tucked into the soil.

AFTERCARE

Keep the herbs well watered, but do not allow them to become waterlogged. At the end of the season, transplant them to a sunny spot in the garden. Depending on your zone, some of these plants will need to be treated as annuals and replanted the following year; others will die down for the winter, but, given space, will increase in size for next summer.

strawberry basket

● *2 hours*

Hanging baskets can be more than just decorative: include edibles in the planting and they can be productive, too. This one has strawberries packed in among bright verbenas, but there are many other edible plants you could include in a hanging basket. Herbs work very well, especially if you add some decorative flowers; chilies can be fun, as can dwarf tomatoes and beans. The trick is to get the young plants in by the end of April (or once there is no more risk of frost), so that they have plenty of time to get established before the summer. You will also need to use generous amounts of fertilizer to compensate for the limited quantity of soil.

ABOVE AND OPPOSITE: *Vermilion verbenas add to the scarlet hues of the strawberries, lending interest to the basket all through the summer. In early summer, the strawberry flowers provide a decorative touch, developing into fruits over the season. The Victorian-style wire basket lends structure to the whole ensemble.*

you will need

Large hanging basket
Coco-fiber hanging basket liner, preferably 'cloverleaf' style
Black trash bag
Scissors
Container compost

Water-retaining gel
Slow-release fertilizer
3 trailing strawberry plants (zones 3–9)
6 *Verbena* × *hybrida* Quartz Series
3 *Verbena* × *hybrida* 'Scarlet'

1 Thoroughly water the plants, and allow them to drain. Place the basket on a large container for support. (If your liner does not have slits, cut six or seven around the edge.) Place the liner in the basket.

2 Using a trowel, fill the basket one-third full with potting mix, then add water-retaining gel, following the manufacturer's recommendations.

3 Add slow-release fertilizer, following the manufacturer's recommendations. Using a trowel, mix the water-retaining gel and slow-release fertilizer into the soil.

4 Cut a piece of black plastic from a trash bag and wrap up one of the white-eyed verbenas. Do this by laying the plant in the middle of the piece of plastic and then wrapping first one side and then the other around it. Make sure the roots are completely covered, so that they are protected during planting.

5 Now pass the root end of the package from the outside of the basket to the inside through one of the slits.

6 Once the roots are safely through the side of the basket, pull the piece of plastic away and carefully bed the roots into the potting mix.

7 In the same way, add the remaining white-eyed verbenas evenly around the basket. Add another layer of soil to fully bed the roots in.

8 Now carefully bed in the three strawberry plants in the top of the basket.

9 Add the three 'Scarlet' verbenas next to the strawberries in the top of the basket. Fill in-between the plants with potting mix, carefully pressing it down firmly with your fingers.

10 Thoroughly water in the planted-up basket, using a fine rose on the watering can.

AFTERCARE

Position the basket in a sheltered, sunny position. Keep well watered while the plants are establishing and during dry periods. Liquid-feed while the strawberries are fruiting. Deadhead the verbenas to encourage repeat flowering; repeat these annuals the following year.

pretty pear tree

● *30 minutes*

If you'd like to grow your own fruit, even if all you have is a patio, there's no reason why you shouldn't do so. Growers are now producing fruit trees on dwarfing root stocks, such as this pear, that are perfectly happy with life in a pot. Like all fruit trees, though, they're a little leggy in their early years, so you might wish to pretty them up a bit. This one has been underplanted with flirty French lavender, which not only displays a mass of charming winged blooms all summer, but keeps its pretty, feathery leaves through the winter, providing all-year interest.

you will need

Large container
1 dwarf pear tree (typically zones 5–8)
Rich potting mix
4 French (or Spanish) lavender (*Lavandula* 'Alexandra') (zones 6–9)
Liquid plant feed

ABOVE LEFT: *A heart-shaped, metal candle holder makes a witty decoration for the pear tree, especially when a "bought" pear takes the place of the candle!*

OPPOSITE: *Dress up your patio fruit trees by underplanting them with something colorful, such as French lavender, and hanging ornaments such as this heart candle holder on their branches. A metal garden bird ornament could be a fun alternative.*

1 Thoroughly water all the plants and allow to drain. Using a trowel, part fill the container with potting mix.

2 Carefully remove the tree from its pot and try it in the container to check for height. Place it in the center. There should be enough space for one lavender in each corner of the container.

3 Remove one lavender plant from its pot and place it in one corner of the container. Its root ball should be about 2 in (5 cm) from the top of the container to allow for topdressing and watering space.

4 Position the other three lavender plants in the container, one at each corner. You may have to put extra soil in each corner underneath the plants.

5 Finally, once all the plants are in position, fill around and between them with more soil, pressing it down firmly with your fingers. Water in, using a liquid feed solution and as per the manufacturer's instructions.

AFTERCARE

Position in a sunny spot and keep watered while the plants establish themselves. This pear tree (Patio Conference) is self fertile, so it will produce fruit on its own, though it may produce more if planted near other pears.

French lavender is not as hardy as the more common *Lavandula angustifolia* varieties, but will survive a mild winter. In zones colder than zone 6 it is best to bring the container indoors— or, if only slightly colder, wrap it in burlap. The lavender flowers should be cut down to leaf level after flowering. In March, you can trim the plants to shape, but do not cut into the woody stems as they may not re-shoot from that level.

handy canes

● *4 hours including drying time*

Many plants, such as scarlet runner beans and tomatoes, need to grow up a vertical support of some kind. In England we like to use traditional "peasticks," which are a byproduct of coppicing hazel, birch, and other woods, but these can be hard to obtain. Bamboo canes—if not quite so picturesque—do the job perfectly well. To make them more attractive, give them a coat of paint and, if available, some decorative safety toppers like those shown here, tied on with raffia. If you can't find safety toppers, use small plant pots (see page 135), painted to match, or some bright-colored duct tape to make the tops more visible and less likely to cause an accident.

LEFT AND OPPOSITE: *Painted in varying blue-green shades, the canes bring a decorative touch to the garden while toning well with all the natural greens of the garden plants.*

you will need

Bamboo canes

Large pieces of newspaper or plastic sheeting to protect your work surface

Can of primer sealer for hard-to-stick surfaces

Selection of bottles

Selection of sample cans of latex paint

Paintbrush

Decorative cane toppers

Raffia—either natural or to tone with the paint

1 Protect your work surface with newspaper or plastic sheeting, then spray each of the canes with the primer sealer. Try to work close to the paper and spray in a downward direction, to avoid spraying any other surfaces.

2 Stand the canes in bottles to allow them to dry thoroughly all around and along their full length.

3 Using the paintbrush and small sample cans of paint in different blue-green hues, paint the full length of the canes.

4 Place a safety topper on the top of each cane. Alternatively, you can wind some colored duct tape around the top of the cane.

5 Finally, cut some lengths of raffia and tie them to each topper, neatly trimming the ends. Or paint some small plant pots to serve as safety toppers.

bird scarers

● *2 hours*

One of the main challenges fruit and vegetable growers face is protecting their produce from garden denizens great and small. Birds love to plunder tender shoots and succulent fruits, so there's always a need for devices to shoo them off humanely . . . and while you're about it, you might as well make it decorative. These bird scarers, made of colored wire hung with tiny bells, look great fun in the vegetable patch. But while we humans love the bright, shiny colors and tinkling bells, it's a decidedly scary combination for birds, who would really rather steer clear!

ABOVE AND OPPOSITE: *Brightly colored wires bring interest to fruit and vegetable patches, especially in spring and early summer, when everything is still very small and green. Make several, mount them on bamboo canes, and let them brighten up whole rows of produce.*

you will need

3 yd (2.8 m) of 12-gauge (2-mm) galvanized steel wire for the spring

1½ yd (1.5 m) of 18-gauge (1-mm) galvanized steel wire for the flower shape

3 yd (2.8 m) loop of 18-gauge (1-mm) green anodized craft wire

9 yd (8.2 m) loop of 23- gauge (0.56-mm) lilac anodized craft wire

1½ yd (1.5 m) fine florist's wire

Wire cutter/pliers

Bamboo cane

Short piece of dowel, slightly thicker than the bamboo

Short piece of thinner dowel

6 small bells

1 Start by winding 12-gauge/2-mm galvanized steel wire (available from garden centers) around the thicker dowel, leaving a "tail" of straight wire before you begin winding. Wind this all the way down the dowel, pull the coil you have made off the end, and continue winding until you have created the length you need. Remove the dowel.

2 Now make the flower shape to go on the top of the bird scarer by shaping the thinner-gauge wire with your fingers. Using 18-gauge/1-mm galvanized steel wire, start by leaving a long "stalk", then make an open spiral of wire for the center of the flower. When the spiral is almost the required size, use your fingers to form bends in the last "round", creating the flower outline.

3 Wind the green craft wire (available from jewelry and craft stores and web sites) around the thinner piece of dowel until you've made a coil long enough to cover the central spiral of the flower. You may need to pull it down the dowel as you go, so that you can carry on winding. Slip the green coil off the dowel.

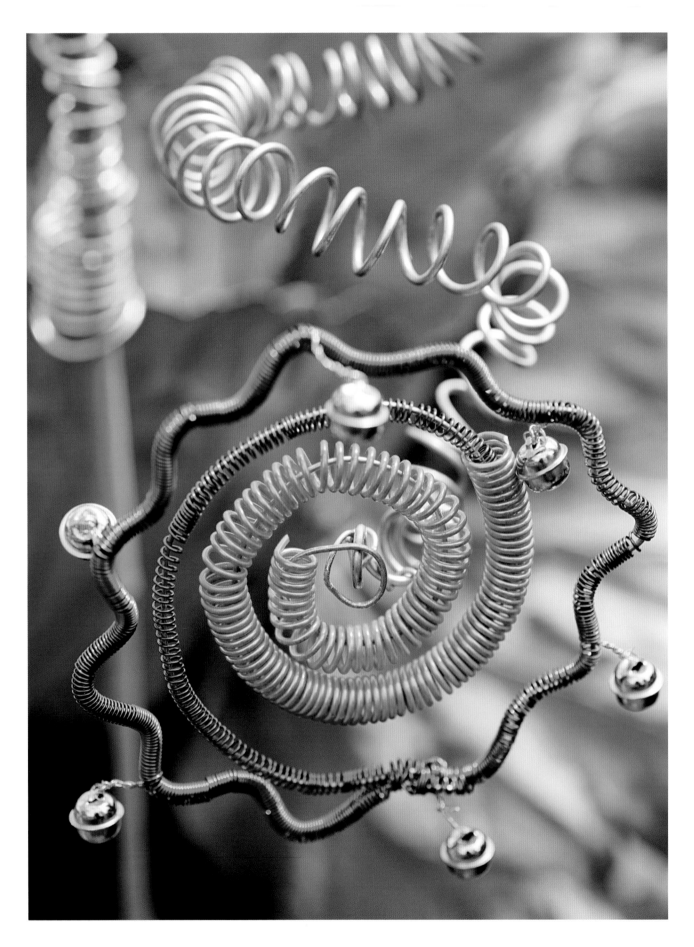

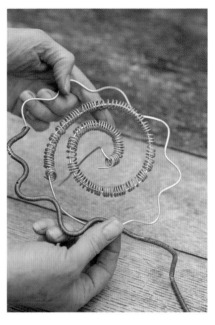

4 Make a lilac coil in the same way, by winding it around a piece of the thickest gauge of wire. Make it long enough to go around all the "petals" of the flower shape.

5 Now slip the green coil onto the flower, feeding it all the way through to the spiral at the center.

6 In the same way, slip the lilac wire coil onto the wiggly part of the flower— the curved "petal" shapes around the outside.

7 Slip a short piece of fine florist's wire into each bell, and wire the bells in place at intervals around the flower.

OPPOSITE: *Follow the instructions to make a green and lilac version of this extrovert flower-like bird scarer.*

8 Slip the flower "stem" into the top of the wire spring that you made in step 1 (see page 164).

9 Fit the other end of the spring over the bamboo cane, winding the "tail" around the cane to fix it on firmly. To use, simply push the cane into the ground.

vintage charm

● *15 minutes*

Trawl secondhand stores and garage sales for vintage containers to turn delicious plantings into something altogether more delightful. This 1960s' enamel clothespin bucket, with its witty polka-dot design, is a lovely foil for some strawberries. It already has a hanger (originally to hang on the clothes line) and drainage holes, which make it the perfect mini hanging basket. The planting brings interest all through the summer, starting with the vibrant green strawberry leaves. Then comes the mass of charming white flowers, followed by the fruit, which drapes prettily over the sides.

you will need

Container
Potting mix
1 strawberry plant
Water-retaining gel
Slow-release fertilizer

LEFT AND OPPOSITE: *This delightful vintage clothespin bucket makes an ideal container, complete with original drainage holes and a handle that incorporates a hook for hanging it on a branch.*

1 Collect everything together, thoroughly water the plants, and let them drain through. Scrub out the container before you plant it up.

2 Using a small trowel, cover the bottom of the container with soil. Add water-retaining gel and slow-release fertilizer, following the manufacturer's instructions.

3 Carefully release the strawberry plant from its pot, and place it in the container. Fill around the plant with soil, firmly pressing it in with your fingers. Water thoroughly.

AFTERCARE
Keep well watered, especially while the plant is fruiting. Pick off any dead leaves, and harvest the fruit when ripe.

ABOVE AND OPPOSITE: *The combination of bright red, ripe chillis and vermilion, bright pink and salmon, planted into an azure blue, glazed container, was still adding a vibrant splash in the garden by the end of September.*

you will need

Glazed container

Potting mix

1 chili plant such as 'Serrano Chilli' or 'Twilight' (zones 5–7)

6 *Celosia Kimono Series (Plumosa Group)*

hot chili mix

● *30 minutes*

By August, the garden is often looking a little past its best. The summer blooms are over, and the greenery is less lush, more overgrown, and dried up. In short, if your garden looks tired by August, don't be surprised. And don't become despondent, either. In a month or two, gentler sunshine, soft rain, and morning dew will perk it up, bringing back the lush greenery, ripening the fruits, and bringing on autumn flowers. But what to do in the meantime? One of the best solutions is to introduce color with red-hot chili peppers and boost the hues by adding other hot tones to the container. In some northern climes, you won't be able to get chili plants until about June, as that's when they're ready to come out from under glass. The chilies might not be red by then, but they will take on color as the summer progresses. For instant color, add *Celosia* to the container. Their brightly colored, chili-shaped, feathery blooms are a great complement to the pepper plants, and they will add vibrancy from June through August and beyond.

1 Collect all the materials together, thoroughly water all the plants, and allow them to drain. If you are reusing the container from last year, scrub it out well to ensure that there are no residual diseases or pests from previous plantings.

2 Place a piece of crock over the drainage hole. Then, using a trowel, part fill the container with potting mix.

3 Carefully release the chili pepper plant from its pot to avoid damaging the roots, then try it in the container. The top of the root ball should be about 2 in (5 cm) from the rim to allow for topdressing and watering space.

4 Now arrange the *Celosia* around the chili pepper plant, easing them into the corners of the container.

5 Finally, pack soil around and between all the plants, pressing it down firmly with your fingers. Thoroughly water in the finished planting.

AFTERCARE

Chilies

Chilies don't thrive below 54°F (12°C) . Put them in a sunny, sheltered spot. They should be watered copiously, then allowed to almost dry out before another drenching. Some experts even wait until they see the leaves wilt a little before watering. Chillis are pretty much left alone by pests, who find the flavor too hot to handle! The chillis can be harvested when they are green or when they are red. In northern zones chillis should be treated as half-hardy annuals. If you want them to survive in winter, cut them to 2in (5cm) and keep them inside at a temperature of not less than 12°C (54°F).

Celosia

Celosia also like plenty of sun. Ideally, they like to be given liquid feed while they are flowering, but the chilies would prefer to do without—so if they are planted together like this, do not feed. This planting was still looking good after two months without feeding.

pretty and tasty

● *30 minutes*

We all love herbs: their heady aroma pervades the garden; their pungent flavors enrich our cooking. But most of them don't do much to enhance the garden visually. We don't want them to flower, because then they lose their flavor. Solution? Plant them with something pretty that will do the flowering for them! Choose a robust plant with a long flowering season, such as this delightful *Erigeron*, whose leaves are similar in color to the thyme, giving a cohesive feel to a container that looks as good as it smells.

you will need

Stone container

Potting mix

3 large thyme plants (zones 6–8)

3 large *Erigeron* 'Wayne Roderick' (zones 6–10)

Cobbles or large pebbles

FAR LEFT AND RIGHT: *Thyme and* Erigeron, *planted together in a rugged stone container set on cobbles, make a delightful, easy-to-look-after focal point in a small town garden.*

1 Collect all the materials together and water thoroughly. Place a layer of soil in the bottom of the container. Next, carefully remove the first thyme from its pot and plant it in the container.

2 Arrange the cobbles around the container to create a rugged display to set off the plants.

3 Plant the other thyme plants, making a good, full display. In the same way, plant the *Erigeron* into the container with the thyme. Carefully pack more soil around and between the plants, pressing it in firmly with your fingers. Water thoroughly.

AFTERCARE

Place in a sunny position and do not allow to dry out. Harvest the thyme as needed. Deadhead the *Erigeron* flowers to encourage repeat blooms.

index

plants for your zone

For the perennial plants recommended in this book, we have included the zones in which they are likely to flourish—for example, "(zones 5–9)." The crucial figure in each case is the lower one, which indicates the coldest zone in which the plant is likely to survive the winter. The upper figure indicates that, for one reason or another, the plant is unlikely to flourish in a zone warmer than that one.

The author has naturally chosen plants that thrive in her own country, England, which has a temperate climate. Many of these will also thrive in northern zones of the United States, but some will not. If a particular species or cultivar falls outside your zone, or if you are unable to obtain it, consult an expert at a local garden center, who should be able to recommend a good substitute.

acknowledgments

My thanks go to my inspired teammate, Debbie, whose gorgeous, vibrant photographs have brought all the projects to life; to Chris for her elegant book design; to Cindy Richards at Cico who came up with the idea in the first place; to Sally, who provided support through the odds and to Dawn who saw it through.

contributors
Thank you, too, to Karin Hossack, who designed and made the elegant stripy pots and extrovert wire bird scarers; The Lobster Pot Café at Felpham for its delightful boat garden (as well as the best breakfasts and better-still dinners) and to Peggy Rooke, who not only let us dig up bits of the garden, but looked after some of the projects as they grew to maturity over the summer.

locations
There were many other generous people who helped to make the book the visual treat that it is, especially those who offered their gardens as locations. In order of appearance:

Dan Cullen at Ginkgo Gardens, Jim Buckland at West Dean Gardens, Peter and Peggy Rooke, Pam Fox, Carrie and Dan Pangbourne, and Karin and Ian Hossack.

For more information:
www.ginkgogardens.co.uk
www.thelobsterpotfelpham.com
www.westdean.org.uk